An Explanation
of
The Common Service

with

Appendices on Christian Hymnody and
Liturgical Colors
and a Glossary of Liturgical Terms

Fifth Edition
Revised and Enlarged

First published in 1908 by the United Lutheran Publication House, Philadelphia.

Reprinted in 2006 by Emmanuel Press
1916 Ridgewood Ave. SE, Grand Rapids, Michigan 49506
www.emmanuelpress.us

Cover artwork by Edward Riojas
10385 Byron Center Ave., Byron Ctr., Michigan 49315
Copyright © 2006 by Emmanuel Press

ISBN 0-9763832-3-3

To the
Young Lutheran who asks
The Meaning of the
Beautiful Liturgy of
His Church

FOREWORD

THE preparation of this little book was begun February 9, 1903. The first edition was issued in four parts, beginning September 29, of the same year. The work was undertaken at the instance of the Luther League of the Allentown District, by a committee appointed for this special purpose. The book was intended for use in the Luther League meetings, as a guide and aid in the study of the Common Service. In its new form it is offered to the Evangelical Lutheran Church in America, for use in the Luther League, the Sunday-school and the home. For League and Bible Class study, it will furnish abundant material for a half year's course of twenty-six lessons.

In the preparation of this Explanation the standard sources and authorities have been consulted. It has been deemed unnecessary to give particular credit for whatever has been adopted from these sources, as the only pretension which the book makes is to a certain unique fitness and convenience for popular use. Whatever seemed well adapted to explain the meaning and the connection of the several parts of the Services of the Church was freely used

In order to give completeness to the work, and to bring out more clearly the beautiful harmony of the parts of the Service which are appointed for the particular Festival or Day, the propria for the Festival of Christmas were selected and have been inserted and examined in their appropriate places in the Service.

5

The Lutheran Church may justly claim that, in the Common Service, she possesses and uses "the completest embodiment of the Common Service of the Christian Church of all ages"; a Service "which may be tendered to all Christians who use a fixed Order, the Service of the future as it has been of the past" (Preface to the Common Service). Should this book be of assistance to any one, in awakening interest, or in developing a better understanding, a more intelligent use, and a higher appreciation of the forms of Divine Worship, as the Church of the Reformation conceives and orders it, the very considerable time and labor which its production has cost will not have been spent in vain.

The second revised and enlarged edition of the Explanation was prepared by four members of the original committee, the Revs. Frederick E. Cooper, Edwin F. Keever, John C. Seegers and Joseph Stump. The Rev. G. Adolph Bruegel, who died in January, 1906 was also a member of the committee, and assisted in the preparation of the first edition; as did the Rev. Paul Z. Strodach, now of Canton, Ohio, who was appointed in his stead.

The present fourth edition has been conformed in text to the new Common Service Book.

An Explanation

of

The Common Service

Introduction

---

1. What is Divine Worship?

Divine Worship in its widest significance includes the observance of every rite or ceremony whereby man believes that God communes with him, and he with God.

2. Distinguish between the true and the false worship of God.

True worship of God is only such as conforms in spirit and expression with God's revelation of Himself. Read John 4:24.

All worship is false which seeks communion with God in ways other than those which He has appointed. False worship is either

(a) The paying of divine honors to false gods, such as idolatry (the Hindoos), nature-worship (the Greeks), ancestor-worship (the Chinese), or

(b) The false worship of the true God. Such is the worship of the hypocrite. Read Matt. 15:7-9; Matt. 7:21-23. Such has become all Jewish worship which was abrogated by the Advent of our Lord.

3. Distinguish between the true worship of God before and after Christ.

Before Christ, the true worship was that of the Jews, temporary, typical, a shadow of good things to come. Since Christ, the true worship is that of the Christians, final, perfect, and the very substance of those things. Read Heb. 1:1, 2; John 1:17 with Heb. 7:18, 19. Also Luke 16:16; Heb. 9:11, 12, 23-26, and Heb. 10:9.

9

4. What is Christian Worship?

It is the outward expression, by the power of the Holy Ghost, of the communion of man with God, through Jesus Christ our Lord.

5. Of what elements does Christian Worship consist?

Christian Worship consists of two elements—the sacramental and the sacrificial.

In the sacramental acts of worship, God speaks to us. In the sacrificial acts, we speak to God. In the sacramental acts, God's grace is exhibited, offered and conveyed. In the sacrificial, man offers to God the service which is due Him.

6. Which are the chief sacramental acts in The Service?

The Declaration of Grace.

The Lessons.

The Sermon.

The Distribution of the Holy Supper.

The Benedictions (The Votum, The Pax, "The body of our Lord," etc., "The Lord bless thee," etc.).

7. Which are the sacrificial acts?

The Confession.

The Prayers.

The Hymns and Canticles.

The Creed.

The Offerings.

NOTE.—The Introit is both sacramental and sacrificial. The Words of Institution are regarded by some as sacramental, by others as sacrificial.

8. In view of the above, what is the proper attitude of the Minister when he conducts the various parts of the worship?

While conducting the sacramental parts of worship, the Minister should face the people, because at such times he stands as the Lord's ambassador and addresses them in His Name. Read II Cor. 5 : 20 (Revised Version).

While conducting the sacrificial parts, the Minister should face the altar, as do the people, since he now addresses the Lord on their behalf and as their leader.

9. Distinguish between private and public worship.

Private worship is the communion of the individual soul with God. Public worship is the common and united worship of believers in the unity of the Body of Christ, as they are assembled in the church.

10. Is this distinction important?

Yes, for there are indispensable elements of true worship in which no one can engage except in common with others. Public worship is, moreover, an Apostolic rule, a permanent institution, and accords with the universal practice of the Church. The writer of the Epistle to the Hebrews most beautifully exhorts to common worship in chapter 10, verses 19 to 25.

11. How did Christian worship become corrupted?

As the teaching of the Church became corrupted, the worship of the Church naturally shared that corruption. Men were taught that their works and prayers, their pilgrimages and fasts atoned for their sins. Christ's work of atonement, and faith in Him were lost to sight. This inevitably led to the perversion of the sacramental element of worship, and the undue exaltation of the priesthood; and the whole service, even the Lord's Supper, came to be regarded as a sacrifice offered to God by the priest on behalf of the people. This was the fundamental error of the Romish Church of the Middle Ages.

12. How did it come to be purified?

The Lutheran Reformers led the way in this work. Just as false teaching developed a corrupt worship, so the restoration of pure doctrine effected the restoration of pure worship. The New Testament teaches that we are saved by grace, not by works. Therefore, as Luther maintained, in true Christian worship the Divine Word and the Holy Supper are not a sacrifice which man offers to God, but means of grace in which God comes to man. Hence the sacramental should be the chief element in the Service, as it is with us.

13. What was the attitude of the non-Lutheran Reformers in revising the Service?

Zwingli, in his first Order of Worship, which he introduced at Zurich, followed Luther's Form of the Mass rather closely; but later he aimed at eliminating from the service all forms which were not directly traceable to New Testament usage. Calvin sought in every way to simplify the Service. He appeared to think that the spiritual and churchly development of fifteen centuries could be swept away by simply ignoring it. His aim was to go back to the foundation principles of the Church as it existed in the days of the Apostles. With this in view, he abandoned everything that could not be justified from Holy Scripture as Apostolic or early Christian. Accordingly, he made of the church a mere house of prayer; the altar became a simple table; statues, pictures, and even the cross had to disappear from the church; music was barely tolerated in the form of simple psalm-singing. Thus, besides the Lord's Supper, the only component parts of the Service were psalm-singing, preaching and prayer. John Knox prepared "The Book of Common Order" for the English congregation at Frankfort, and it afterwards became the established order of worship in Scotland, and remained such for nearly a century. This order was approved by John Calvin, and was used by the English congregation at Geneva.

14. Is the Lutheran conception of worship held by the other Protestant churches also?

No, for in those churches chief emphasis is laid upon the *sacrificial* element. This is done to such an extent, that even such sacramental ordinances as the Lord's Supper and Baptism are regarded as the Christian's own acts of worship, rather than as means through which God offers and bestows His grace.

15. What is the Anglican (Episcopal) conception of worship?

It varies with the High and Low Church tendencies. The High Church conception is Romish, while the Low Church is Calvinistic.

16. What was the relation of the English Reformers to the Lutheran in the work of revising the ancient Service?

The Lutheran revision of the Service, issued in many editions, in many states and cities, had been fully tested by more than *twenty years* of continuous use before the revision made by the English Church, first issued in the Prayer Book of Edward the Sixth, 1549. The Latin Missals, from which the English translations were made, agreed almost entirely with the Missals from which the German translations had been made. Archbishop Cranmer, the head of the commission which prepared the first English Prayer Book, spent a year and a half in Germany in conference with Lutheran theologians and princes, and was thoroughly familiar with the Lutheran Service. Two Lutheran professors, who were called to the English Universities, took part in the formation of the Prayer Book. During the years 1535 to 1549 there had been many embassies and conferences between the English and the Lutheran rulers and theologians concerning these matters.

17. In the reformation of the Service, who led the Lutheran movement?

Luther, who in the year 1523 published his treatise "Of the Order of Divine Service in the Congregation," and later in the same year, his "Form of the Mass"; and John Bugenhagen, chief pastor at Wittenberg, who published an "Order of Christian Mass," in 1524. For other early Lutheran Orders, see the Preface to The Common Service.

18. What were the principal changes which the Lutheran Reformers introduced?

While the Lutheran Reformers retained all that was deemed sound and Scriptural in the Latin Mass, the work of purification required some radical changes. The chief change was in the view which was taken of the Mass. What had been wrongly regarded as a sacrifice, was now understood in its true significance as a sacrament. The Liturgy was translated into the language of the people; the Sermon was assigned greater importance; all that was contrary to Scripture was removed; church song was given a new and higher place; a few things were added, such as the General Prayer and the Exhortation before the Communion.

19. What is the Common Service?

It is the typical Lutheran Service of the Sixteenth Century, adapted for the use of English-speaking Churches.

20. Why is it called the Common Service?

(a) Because it embodies the common worship of the pure Christian Church of all ages.

(b) Because of the rule which governed its preparation, namely, "The Common Consent of the Pure Lutheran Liturgies of the Sixteenth Century."

(c) Because it was prepared in common by three of the general bodies of the Lutheran Church in America, namely, The United Synod of the South, The General Synod, and The General Council. These bodies are now united and known as "The United Lutheran Church in America." It is also used in common in all parts of the English Lutheran Church.

21. What obligation is there upon Lutheran Congregations to use a Common Service?

According to the Lutheran Confessions, there can be no binding obligation, but there is a strong moral and churchly obligation; for these same Confessions say: "It is pleasing to us that, for the sake of unity and good order, universal rites be observed."

22. What forms of worship are included in the Common Service?

The Service or The Communion.
Matins.
Vespers.

23. What are the distinguishing marks of these several Services?

The Communion is the chief Service of the Lord's Day, and by common consent its most appropriate time is near the middle of the day. Matins for the morning, and Vespers for the evening, are minor services for daily use.

The Communion we trace directly to our Lord's institution of the Holy Supper, and to the obedience of the first believers as "they continued steadfastly in the Apostles' doctrine and fellowship, and in the breaking of bread, and in prayers" (Acts 2:42). Matins and Vespers we trace to the daily worship of the early Christians, which they in turn inherited from the Synagogue of the Jews.

Order of
The Service or The Communion

Order of The Service or The Communion

24. **What name is given to our principal Service?**

The Service or The Communion. German: Haupt-Gottesdienst (Chief Service). Swedish: Högmässa (High Mass). Norwegian and Danish: Höimesse (High Mass). The term Mass is authorized by the Augsburg Confession (Art. XXIV).

25. **Should it be used at any other than a morning hour?**

Certainly. It should always be used when only one service is held on a Sunday; and also whenever the Communion is administered.

26. **What private preparation should the Christian make before attending the Service on the Lord's Day?**

He should devoutly read the Introit, Collect, Epistle and Gospel, of the Day.

27. **What should be the first act of the worshiper upon entering the House of God?**

He should bow his head in silent prayer, asking God to prepare his heart for worship.

A FORM OF SILENT PRAYER.

O God, Send Thy Holy Spirit into my heart, that He may enable me to receive the gift of grace which Thou hast for me this Day, through Jesus Christ, my Lord. Amen.

19

28. Why may a hymn of invocation of the Holy Ghost precede the Service?

Because it is only by the Holy Ghost that we can render worship to God through Christ.   I Cor. 12: 3; Eph. 2: 18.

———

IN the Name of the Father, and of the Son, and of the Holy Ghost.

29. Why does the Service begin in the name of the Triune God?

Because God has revealed Himself as Father, Son, and Holy Ghost; and it is by His authority that the Minister proclaims the Gospel, and for His worship that a Christian congregation assembles.   Compare Ex. 3: 13, 14, and Matt. 18: 20.

30. Why does the congregation respond Amen?

Amen means *So be it.*   By its use here the congregation accepts and confirms the words of the Minister.

The Preparation*

The Confession of Sins

31. What is the purpose of the preparatory Confession?

It prepares the hearts of both Minister and congregation for communion with God. Without the sincere confession of sin God does not bestow His grace upon us; nor does He accept our sacrifices of prayer, praise and thanksgiving.

32. Name the several parts of the Preparation.

    I.   The Exhortation.
    II.   The Versicle.
    III.   The Confession of Sins.
    IV.   The Prayer for Grace.
    V.   The Declaration of Grace.

The Exhortation

BELOVED in the Lord! Let us draw near with a true heart, and confess our sins unto God our Father, beseeching Him, in the Name of our Lord Jesus Christ, to grant us forgiveness.

33. What is suggested in this Exhortation?

"Let us draw near," i. e., The entrance to the Divine Sanctuary is always open to us, our great High Priest and Reconciler being there to receive us. This approach is the mark of a true believer. Read Heb. 10: 22.

"With a true heart," i. e., Properly prepared to confess; not

---

*When The Service is immediately preceded by the Service of Confession and Absolution, it should begin with the Introit, The Preparation being omitted.

hypocritical or double-minded; conscious of our depravity and failings.   Read Psalm 32:5 and I John 1:8, 9.

"And confess our sins," etc.   This we do in the following Confession.

"Beseeching Him . . . forgiveness."   This we do in the Prayer for Grace.

The Versicle

Our help is in the Name of the Lord.
Who made heaven and earth.
I said I will confess my transgressions unto the Lord.
And Thou forgavest the iniquity of my sin.

34. What is the office of a Versicle?

Versicles are short passages of Scripture intended to incite the worshipers to devotion and to suggest the central thought of what follows.   Here the Versicle encourages us to approach.

35. Where is this Versicle found?

In Psalms 124 and 32.

36. What is indicated in the Versicle?

1.   From Whom our help comes.
2.   God's power to help.
3.   The condition on which help is granted.
4.   A word of God assuring help.

The Confession

ALMIGHTY God, our Maker and Redeemer, we poor sinners confess unto Thee, that we are by nature sinful and unclean, and that we have sinned against Thee by thought, word, and deed.

Wherefore we flee for refuge to Thine infinite mercy, seeking and imploring Thy grace, for the sake of our Lord Jesus Christ.

37. What is contained in the Confession propei?

I. A confession to God by the Minister for himself and the congregation,

    1. Of original sin,

    2. Of actual sin in thought, word and deed.

II. An avowal to God that we flee from this sin to His mercy, seeking His grace through Christ.

The Prayer for Grace

O MOST merciful God, Who hast given Thine Only-begotten Son to die for us, have mercy upon us, and for His sake grant us remission of all our sins: and by Thy Holy Spirit increase in us true knowledge of Thee, and of Thy will, and true obedience to Thy Word, to the end that by Thy grace we may come to everlasting life, through Jesus Christ our Lord. Amen.

38. What is contained in the Prayer for Grace?

I. The ground of this prayer—the death of Christ.

II. The petitions of this prayer,

    1. For mercy.

    2. For forgiveness,

    3. For an increase: (a) of the knowledge of God and His will, (b) of true obedience to His Word.

III. The object of this prayer—that through God's grace we may come to everlasting life.

The Declaration of Grace

ALMIGHTY God, our heavenly Father, hath had mercy upon us, and hath given His Only Son to die for us, and for His sake forgiveth us all our sins. To them that believe on His Name, He giveth power to become the sons of God, and bestoweth upon them His Holy Spirit. He that believeth and is baptized, shall be saved. Grant this, O Lord, unto us all. Amen.

39. What is contained in the Declaration of Grace?

It contains the whole order of salvation, and hence becomes a complete answer to the Prayer for Grace. It declares:

I. That God has always had mercy upon us, and therefore gave His Son to die for us.

II. That for Christ's sake He now forgives us all our sins.

III. That to those who believe He grants the increase of knowledge and obedience for which they pray, by giving them power to become the sons of God, and by giving unto them His Holy Spirit.

40. With what does this Declaration close?

With the prayer that the Holy Spirit may work this faith in *us,* and thus apply to *each heart* the forgiveness which Christ has obtained for it.

These words ("Grant this, O Lord, unto us all") resolve what precedes into a prayer for the forgiveness of the confessing penitent, which was the earliest form of the Absolution (precative). The form in the Order of Public Confession is declarative ("I declare unto you," etc.). The form used in the Roman Church is indicative ("I absolve thee").

41. What is the significance of the Amen here?

It affirms our belief that God has forgiven our sins. Amen: Yea, yea, it shall be so.

The Service Proper

---

42. What are the general divisions of the Service?

    I.   The Office of the Word.

    II. The Holy Supper.

The Office of the Word

43. Of what is the Office of the Word composed?

    Of three parts, viz:

      I.   The Psalmody: Introit to Gloria in Excelsis.

      II. The Word: Salutation to Votum.

      III. The Offerings: Offertory to The Hymn.

Part 1.—The Psalmody

44. With what does the Office of the Word begin?

    With the Introit.

The Introit

(CHRISTMAS.)

UNTO us a Child is born, unto us a Son is given: and the government shall be upon His shoulder.

And His Name shall be called Wonderful, Counsellor, the Mighty God: the Everlasting Father, the Prince of Peace.

Ps. O sing unto the Lord a new song: for He hath done marvellous things.

Glory be to the Father, etc.

45. What is the origin of the Introit?

INTROIT comes from the Latin *introitus,* meaning beginning or entrance. It is so called, either because originally it was chanted as the Minister entered the church, or because it is the beginning or entrance of the Service.

It takes its rise from the use of the Psalms with which the Service in the Synagogue began, and in all probability the Service of the Apostolic church also. Read Psalm 100.

46. Of what does the Introit consist?

It consists of the Psalm-verse with its Antiphon and the Gloria Patri.

47. What is the meaning of the word Antiphon?

Antiphon means "voice answering voice," and refers to the responsive singing of verses, as was common in the ancient Church.

48. What is the office of the Antiphon?

The Antiphon announces, in a brief passage of Scripture, the leading thought of the Day, and brings the Psalm into proper relation with the Day's Service. For example, in the Introit for Christmas, the Antiphon announces the birth of Christ.

The thought of the Day is emphasized by the repetition of the Antiphon after the Gloria Patri, when the Introit is sung.

49. Explain the use of the Psalm-verse in the Introit.

It is a single verse which has survived the ancient custom of singing an entire psalm at the beginning of the Service. In it the Church appropriates and celebrates, in psalmody, the Gospel fact which is proclaimed for that day in the Antiphon.

50. Why does the Introit include the Gloria Patri?

Because most of the Introits are from the Psalms, and the addition of the Gloria Patri fundamentally distinguishes the use of the Psalter in the New Testament Church from its use in the Synagogue. The Messianic references in the Psalms Jesus declares to have been written concerning Himself (Luke 24:44); and in the confession of that truth, the Christian Church has always concluded the Psalms with this ascription of praise to the Holy Trinity.

Thus the Church perpetuates the confession of the co-eternal Godhead of our Lord and the Holy Ghost, with the Father, which was denied in the controversies of the fourth century.

The Kyrie

Lord, have mercy upon us.
Christ, have mercy upon us.
Lord, have mercy upon us.

51. What is the meaning of the word Kyrie?

It is a Greek word and means, O Lord.

NOTE.—Such titles as Gloria Patri and Gloria in Excelsis from the Latin, and Kyrie from the Greek, are the first words in those languages of the parts of the Service which they name. Psalms and even books, in ancient times, were named by the first word or words.

52. What is the office of the Kyrie?

The congregation, realizing its infirmity from indwelling sin, calls upon God for that grace which has been announced and offered in the Introit.

53. Why is the prayer thrice uttered?

Because the grace for which it asks is from God the Father, through the Son, by the Holy Spirit.

54. By what is this cry for mercy succeeded?

By the Gloria in Excelsis.

This part of the Service strikingly reproduces the order of events related in Luke 18: 35-43.

There the blind man in his misery cried for mercy. So do we in the Kyrie.

He cried persistently. We utter the same prayer three times.

His prayer was answered. Our petitions are likewise granted.

Then he and "all the people with him" glorified and gave praise unto God. So our Kyrie is followed by Gloria in Excelsis.

The Gloria in Excelsis

GLORY be to God on high, and on earth peace, good will toward men. We praise Thee, we bless Thee, we worship Thee, we glorify Thee, we give thanks to Thee for Thy great glory, O Lord God, heavenly King, God the Father Almighty.

O Lord, the Only-begotten Son, Jesus Christ; O Lord God, Lamb of God, Son of the Father, that takest away the sin of the world, have mercy upon us. Thou

that takest away the sin of the world, receive our prayer. Thou that sittest at the
right hand of God the Father, have mercy
upon us.

For Thou only art holy; Thou only art
the Lord; Thou only, O Christ, with the
Holy Ghost, art most high in the glory of
God the Father. Amen.

55. What is the Gloria in Excelsis?

It is one of the oldest morning hymns of the Christian
Church—a hymn of adoration, celebrating God's glory as manifested in the merciful gift of His Son. It is so called from the
first words of the Latin version, meaning literally, "Glory in
the Highest."

56. By whom and when were the opening words sung?

By the Angels at the birth of Christ (Luke 2 : 14).

57. What does Luther say of this part of the Gloria?

"It did not grow; nor was it made on earth; it came down
from heaven."

58. How may the contents of this hymn be outlined?

    I. Adoration of God the Father,
        (a) In the words of the Angels,
        (b) In a rich outburst of praise and thanksgiving in the
            words of the Church.
   II. Adoration of God the Son,
        By acknowledging Him as the Lord, the Only-begotten
          Son, the Christ, God, the Lamb of God.

III.   Petition to God the Son,
       (a) As the One Who procures mercy, by taking away
          the sin of the world;
       (b) As the One Who dispenses mercy, sitting at the
          right hand of God, the Father.

IV.   Praise to God the Son,
      In a three-fold ascription of equal holiness, power, and
      glory with the Father and the Holy Ghost, as the rea-
      son for our prayer and praise.

Part II.—The Word

59. What is the nature of Part II?

In this part we have, through the administration of the Divine Word, the actual bestowal of the grace which, in the first part, has been announced in the Introit, invoked in the Kyrie, and celebrated in the Gloria in Excelsis.

The Salutation and Response

The Lord be with you.
And with thy spirit.

60. What is the significance of the Salutation at the opening of this part of the Service?

It marks the transition to the second part, and introduces the Collect of the Day. Pastor and people pray for each other, invoking the presence of the Lord Who comes to men through His Word. In the Church of the Middle Ages the Salutation and Response introduced every main part of the Service.

The Collect

(CHRISTMAS DAY.)

GRANT, we beseech Thee, Almighty God, that the new birth of Thine Only-begotten Son in the flesh may set us free who are held in the old bondage under the yoke of sin; through the same, Jesus Christ, Thy Son our Lord, Who liveth and reigneth with Thee and the Holy Ghost, ever one God, world without end. Amen.

61. What is the Collect of the Day?

It is a brief prayer which varies with the festivals and seasons of the Church Year.

62. Why is the Collect so called?

Probably because it is the united or collected prayer of the entire congregation, or because it collects and concentrates the thought of Gospel and Epistle. The term is derived from the Latin *Collecta* and *Collectio*.

63. What is the structure of the Collect?

In its full form it has five parts: (a) The invocation. (b) The antecedent reason. (c) The petition. (d) The benefit desired. (e) The doxology. The antecedent reason and the benefit desired are often wanting.

64. Cite examples.

	Ash Wednesday	VIII Trinity	VII Trinity	Sunday after Ascension
Invocation	Almighty and Everlasting God,	Lord,	O God,	Almighty, everlasting God .
Antecedent reason	Who hatest nothing that thou hast made and dost forgive the sins of all those who are penitent		Whose never-failing Providence ordereth all things both in heaven and earth .	
Petition	Create and make in us new and contrite hearts,	Grant to us, we beseech Thee, the Spirit to think and do always such things as are right ;	We humbly beseech Thee to put away from us all hurtful things, and to give us those things which be profitable for us ;	Make us to have always a devout will towards Thy Majesty with a pure heart ;
Benefit desired	that we, worthily lamenting our sins, and acknowledging our wretchedness, may obtain of Thee, the God of all mercy, perfect remission and forgiveness ;	hat we, who cannot do anything that is good without Thee, may by Thee be enabled to live according to Thy will ,		
Doxology	through Jesus Christ Thy Son our Lord who liveth and reigneth with Thee and the Holy Ghost, ever one God, world without end.	through Jesus Christ, thy Son, our Lord, etc.	through Jesus Christ, Thy Son, our Lord, etc.	through Jesus Christ, Thy Son, our Lord, etc.

For variations of the Doxology, see rubrics under Collects and Prayers.

65. By whom should the Collect be said?

The rubric directs the minister to read it; but since it is the prayer of all, the congregation should join the Minister either silently or in a subdued voice. This is indicated by the summons, "Let us pray," and by the Amen, which the congregation is directed to sing or say at the end of the Collect.

66. What is the office of the Collect of the Day?

It serves to prepare the congregation for the reception of the special Word of the Day, now about to be read. In it pastor and people pray for the particular grace which that Word offers and conveys.

67. When was the entire series of Introits, Collects, Epistles and Gospels, as retained in the Lutheran Service, completed?

In the reign of Charlemagne (800 A. D.).

68. How long have our Collects been in use?

There are few, if any, that have not been in use for more than twelve hundred years.

69. What is to be said of the wide use of these Collects?

Most of them are now in use in the Lutheran Churches of Germany, Denmark, Norway, Sweden, the United States and throughout the world; in the Church of England throughout the British Empire; in the Protestant Episcopal Church in America; and (in the Latin language) in the Roman Catholic Church.

The Epistle

(CHRISTMAS.)

Titus 2: 11-14.

For the grace of God that bringeth salvation hath appeared to all men, teaching us that, denying ungodliness and worldly lusts, we should live soberly, righteously, and godly, in this present world; looking for that blessed hope, and the glorious appearing of the great God and our Saviour Jesus Christ; who gave himself for us, that he might redeem us from all iniquity, and purify unto himself a peculiar people, zealous of good works.

70. Where do we find the petition of the Collect answered?

In the Epistle and the Gospel of the Day, which, with the Sermon, constitute the chief part of the Office of the Word.

71. May other Scripture lessons be read?

Yes. But they should be in harmony with the Gospel of the

Day, and, as the rubric directs, they should be read before the Epistle. The Epistle and Gospel should always be read.

72. What is the meaning of the word Epistle?

An epistle is a letter. The first Scripture of the Day is called The Epistle, because it is usually taken from the Letters of the New Testament.

73. What is The Epistle?

The Epistle is the Word which the Holy Spirit addresses to believers through the Apostle, and in which are set forth the faith and life which should characterize them. In the Epistle for Christmas, Paul tells us what the birth of Christ means to us, and describes the manner of life which should follow from our knowledge of this great fact.

The Hallelujah
Hallelujah!

74. Why is Hallelujah sung in response to the Epistle?

Hallelujah is a Hebrew word meaning "Praise the Lord." It is the expression of joy with which the people of God have always received His Word.

NOTE.—Hallelujah occurs frequently in the Book of Psalms from Psalm 104 onwards, and four times in Revelation 19. It was in frequent and general use among early Christians. Plowmen shouted it while at work. Sailors used it as a word of encouragement while plying the oar. Soldiers used it as a battle-cry. When Christians met on Easter morning, "Alleluia, the Lord is risen!" was their salutation. It passed early into frequent liturgical use in all parts of the church, especially in connection with psalms and hymns.

75. What may be used in addition to the Hallelujah at this point of the Service?

As suggested by the rubric, the proper Sentence may be sung with the Hallelujah, or after it a hymn may be sung by the Congregation.

Or, after the Hallelujah Sentence, special choir music may be sung; but it must be in harmony with the thought of the Day. Such music, at this place, serves the purpose of a *gradual,* which anciently was a Psalm sung from the steps (gradus) of the pulpit, or of the altar, as a response to the Epistle. Special music at any other place in the Service should be discountenanced.

76. Is the Hallelujah ever omitted?

As the rubric states, the Hallelujah is to be omitted in the Passion Season (Septuagesima to Good Friday).

The Gospel

(CHRISTMAS.)

Luke 2: 1-14.

AND it came to pass in those days, that there went out a decree from Cæsar Augustus, that all the world should be taxed. (And this taxing was first made when Cyrenius was governor of Syria.) And all went to be taxed, every one into his own city. And Joseph also went up from Galilee, out of the city of Nazareth, into Judæa, unto the city of David, which is called Bethlehem; (because he was of the house and lineage of David:) to be taxed with Mary his espoused wife, being great with child. And so it was, that, while they were there, the days were accomplished that she should be delivered. And she brought forth her firstborn son,

and wrapped him in swaddling clothes,
and laid him in a manger; because there
was no room for them in the inn. And
there were in the same country shepherds
abiding in the field, keeping watch over
their flock by night. And, lo, the angel
of the Lord came upon them, and the glory
of the Lord shone round about them: and
they were sore afraid. And the angel said
unto them, Fear not: for, behold I bring
you good tidings of great joy, which shall
be to all people. For unto you is born
this day in the city of David a Saviour,
which is Christ the Lord. And this shall
be a sign unto you; ye shall find the babe
wrapped in swaddling clothes, lying in a
manger. And suddenly there was with
the angel a multitude of the heavenly host
praising God, and saying, Glory to God in
the highest, and on earth peace, good will
toward men.

77. What point of the Service do we now approach?

The summit of the Office of the Word, namely the Gospel
of the Day.

78. How is this prominence of the Gospel emphasized?

By the Sentences with which the reading of the Gospel is
accompanied, and by the rising of the congregation to hear it.

79. Why does the congregation sing "Glory be to Thee, O Lord" after the Gospel is announced?

In order to express its joy over the prospect of hearing the
blessed Word of Christ Himself.

80. What is the Gospel of the Day?

It is the Good Tidings proclaimed by the Holy Spirit through the Evangelist, in which the saving word and work of Christ, commemorated that day, are set forth. As Christmas commemorates the birth of Christ, the Gospel of that day is the account, from St. Luke, of the Nativity.

81. How does the congregation receive the Gospel?

By singing "Praise be to Thee, O Christ" it glorifies and praises Him for the blessed news.

The Creed

The Nicene Creed.

I BELIEVE in one God, the Father Almighty, Maker of heaven and earth, And of all things visible and invisible.

And in one Lord Jesus Christ, the Only-begotten Son of God, Begotten of His Father before all worlds, God of God, Light of Light, Very God of very God, Begotten, not made, Being of one substance with the Father, By whom all things were made; Who, for us men, and for our salvation, came down from heaven, And was incarnate by the Holy Ghost of the Virgin Mary, And was made man; And was crucified also for us under Pontius Pilate. He suffered and was buried; And the third day He rose again, according to the Scriptures; And ascended into heaven, And sitteth on the right hand of the Father; And He shall come again with glory to judge both the quick and the dead; Whose kingdom shall have no end.

And I believe in the Holy Ghost, The Lord and Giver of Life, Who proceedeth from the Father and the Son, Who with the Father and the Son together is worshiped and glorified, Who spake by the Prophets. And I believe one holy Christian and Apostolic Church. I acknowledge one Baptism for the remission of sins; And I look for the Resurrection of the dead; And the Life of the world to come. Amen.

The Apostles' Creed.

I BELIEVE in God the Father Almighty, Maker of heaven and earth.

And in Jesus Christ His only Son, our Lord; Who was conceived by the Holy Ghost, Born of the Virgin Mary; Suffered under Pontius Pilate, Was crucified, dead, and buried; He descended into hell; The third day He rose again from the dead; He ascended into heaven, And sitteth on the right hand of God the Father Almighty; From thence He shall come to judge the quick and the dead.

I believe in the Holy Ghost; The holy Christian Church, the Communion of Saints; The Forgiveness of sins; The Resurrection of the body; And the Life everlasting. Amen.

82. What is a Creed?

A statement of what one believes. The word is derived from the Latin *Credo,* I believe.

83. Why have we a Creed in the Service?

Because it is necessary to state publicly our acceptance of the truths of God's Word. The most appropriate place for such a confession of faith is in the principal Service. Matt. 10: 32; 16: 15-18; Rom. 10: 9.

84. Why is a Creed recited at this point in the Service?

In it the congregation owns its acceptance of the Word of God just read, and recalls and confesses in a brief summary the whole faith of the Gospel, a part of which is brought to its attention on that day.

85. How does the congregation confess its faith?

By the use of the Nicene or Apostles' Creed—the most ancient creeds of the Christian Church. The Nicene Creed is preferred because it is a fuller statement of the faith, especially respecting the Person of Christ. For this reason it is required when the Communion is administered.

86. What is the Nicene Creed?

It is that confession of faith or summary of Gospel teaching which was developed in the Eastern Church from the baptismal commission—Matt. 28: 19.

NOTE.—The first and second articles of the Nicene Creed were adopted A. D. 325 by an assembly of 318 bishops, at Nicaea in Bithynia, Asia. The third article was adopted by the Council of Constantinople in 381 A. D. The second article was formulated for the express purpose of defining the true doctrine concerning the divinity of Christ, over against the teaching of Arius that Jesus was not the eternal Son of God, co-equal with the Father.

87. What is the Apostles' Creed?

It is that confession of faith or summary of Gospel teaching which was developed more especially in the Western Church.

NOTE.—It took its name from an old tradition that it was composed by the Twelve Apostles, each contributing a sentence. This theory is rejected by all but Roman Catholics. Like other early creeds, the Apostles' Creed grew into its present form from the baptismal commission (Matt. 28:19), until about the year 750 A. D., after which no more changes were made. It has been commonly accepted from the most ancient times. It is called the Baptismal Creed, because universally used in the Baptismal Service.

The Sermon

88. Why may a hymn precede the Sermon?

To prepare the hearts of the people for the preaching of the Word.

89. What should be the character of this hymn?

It should be appropriate to the Day, and accord with the Sermon.

90. What is the Sermon?

It is the explanation and application of the Word which has been read.

91. Why should the Sermon harmonize with the Lessons?

The unity of the Service demands it. To introduce any other topic than one suggested by the thought of the Day throws the whole Service into confusion.

The Votum

THE peace of God, which passeth all understanding, keep your hearts and minds through Christ Jesus.

92. Where in the Scripture is the Votum found?

In St. Paul's Epistle to the Philippians, chapter 4, verse 7.

93. What is the Votum?

It is the benediction after the Sermon, assuring the believing worshipers that the peace of God, in Christ Jesus, offered and bestowed in the preached Word, will keep their hearts and minds in true faith unto everlasting life.

The Votum appropriately concludes and sums up Part II of the Office of the Word.

Part 111.—The Offerings

94. Of what does the third part of the Office of the Word consist?

Of our offerings to God.

95. Why should the Offerings form a part of The Service?

Our faith must show itself in works. The reception of God's richest gift constrains us to give Him what we can.

96. What can we give Him?

Nothing that will atone for our sins. But if we have accepted the great Atonement which Christ has made by offering Himself for us, we shall have grace to offer ourselves, our substance, and our sacrifices of prayer, praise and thanksgiving. With such offerings God is well pleased.

The Offertory

I.

THE sacrifices of God are a broken spirit: a broken and a contrite heart, O God, Thou wilt not despise.

Do good in Thy good pleasure unto Zion: Build Thou the walls of Jerusalem.

Then shalt Thou be pleased with the sacrifices of righteousness: with burnt-offering and whole burnt-offering.

II.

CREATE in me a clean heart, O God:
    and renew a right spirit within me.
Cast me not away from Thy presence:
and take not Thy Holy Spirit from me.
Restore unto me the joy of Thy salvation: and uphold me with Thy free Spirit.

97. Whence are the Offertories in the Common Service taken?

From the 51st Psalm.

98. What is the purpose of the Offertory?

It is an evidence that the Word, just heard, has been appropriated by us and has become effective in us. In the Offertory
we offer ourselves to God that He may cleanse our hearts from
sin, deepen our faith, and prepare us for the reception of the
Visible Word in the Holy Sacrament.

The Offering

99. What act of worship follows the singing of the Offertory?

The offering of the fruit of our labors in the money which we
give for the support of the Church and her Ministry, for the
Poor, for Home and Foreign Missions, for Education, for Or-
phanages and other forms of Christian benevolence.

The General Prayer

ALMIGHTY and most merciful God, the Father
    of our Lord Jesus Christ: We give Thee
thanks for all Thy goodness and tender mercies,
especially for the gift of Thy dear Son, and for the
revelation of Thy will and grace; and we beseech
Thee so to implant Thy Word in us, that, in good

and honest hearts, we may keep it, and bring forth fruit by patient continuance in well doing.

Most heartily we beseech Thee so to rule and govern Thy Church universal, that it may be preserved in the pure doctrine of Thy saving word, whereby faith toward Thee may be strengthened, and charity increased in us toward all mankind.

Send forth Thy light and Thy truth unto the uttermost parts of the earth. Raise up faithful pastors and missionaries to preach the Gospel in our own land and to all nations; and guide, protect, and prosper them in all their labors.

Bless, we pray Thee, the institutions of the Church; its colleges, its seminaries, and all its schools; that they may send forth men and women to serve Thee, in the Ministry of the Word, the Ministry of Mercy, and all the walks of life.

Let the light of Thy Word ever shine within our homes. Keep the children of the Church in the covenant which Thou hast made with them in Holy Baptism; and grant all parents grace to bring them up in faith toward Thee and in obedience to Thy will.

Grant also health and prosperity to all that are in authority, especially to the President [and Congress] of the United States, the Governor [and Legislature] of this Commonwealth, and to all our Judges and Magistrates; and endue them with grace to rule after Thy good pleasure, to the maintenance of righteousness, and to the hindrance and punishment of wickedness, that we may lead a quiet and peaceable life, in all godliness and honesty.

All who are in trouble, want, sickness, anguish of labor, peril of death, or any other adversity, especially those who are in suffering for Thy Name and for Thy truth's sake, comfort, O God, with Thy Holy Spirit, that they may receive and acknowledge their afflictions as the manifestation of Thy fatherly will.

And although we have deserved Thy righteous wrath and manifold punishments, yet, we entreat Thee, O most merciful Father, remember not the sins of our youth, nor our many transgressions; but out of Thine unspeakable goodness, grace and mercy, defend us from all harm and danger of body and soul. Preserve us from false and pernicious doctrine, from war and bloodshed, from plague and pestilence, from all calamity by fire and water, from hail and tempest, from failure of harvest and from famine, from anguish of heart and despair of Thy mercy, and from an evil death. And in every time of trouble, show Thyself a very present Help, the Saviour of all men, and especially of them that believe.

Cause also the needful fruits of the earth to prosper, that we may enjoy them in due season. Give success to all lawful occupations on land and sea, to all pure arts and useful knowledge; and crown them with Thy blessing.

Here special Supplications, Intercessions, and Prayers may be made.

These, and whatsoever other things Thou wouldest have us ask of Thee, O God, vouchsafe unto us for the sake of the bitter sufferings and death of Jesus Christ, Thine only Son, our Lord and Saviour, Who liveth and reigneth with Thee and the Holy Ghost, ever one God, world without end.

Then shall the minister, and the congregation say

The Lord's Prayer.

100. What announcement may be made before the General Prayer?

The Minister shall make mention of any special petitions, intercessions or thanksgivings which may have been requested. He may also make mention of the death of any member of the congregation. (Rubric.)

101. What is offered in the General Prayer?

The fruit of our lips in thanksgiving and petition.

102. Why is it called the General Prayer?

Because in it we pray for all possible blessings to be bestowed not only upon us, but upon all sorts and conditions of men.

103. How long has this prayer been in use?

It was used in almost its present form in 1553. Its origin may be found in the Apostolic injunction that supplications, prayers, intercessions and giving of thanks be made for all men. I Tim. 2: I, 2.

104. Outline the contents of the General Prayer.

The Address, to God, as our Father in Christ.

A General Thanksgiving for all blessings.

A Special Thanksgiving for the gift of Christ and of the Word.

A Petition that the Word may be fruitful in us.

For the Church.

Pastors and People.

Purity of Doctrine.
Strengthening of Faith.
Increase of Love.
For the State.
Rulers, Legislators and Judges.
Good Government and Social Order.
For Enemies.
Reconciliation.
For the Afflicted.
All Sufferers.
Especially those who suffer for Righteousness' sake.
That all may recognize God's Providence in their Afflictions.
For the Forgiveness of all Sins, and
Preservation against all Evil,
Spiritual, Moral, and Bodily.
For
The Products of Nature.
Christian Education.
Every proper Occupation.
Pure Arts, and useful Sciences.
Special Petitions.
(See Question No. 100.)
Conclusion.
All the Thanksgivings, Intercessions and
Petitions of this Prayer are offered through Jesus Christ
our Saviour.

105. May other prayers be used?

If there be no Communion, the Litany, or a selection from the Collects and Prayers may be used (Rubric).

In the Liturgy prepared in 1748, by Muhlenberg and his co-laborers, this rubric appears: "The sermon being concluded, nothing else shall be read than the appointed Church-prayer here following, or the Litany instead of it by way of change; and nothing but necessity shall occasion its omission." This same rubric appears in the printed Liturgy of 1786.

106. Are the prayers of the Common Service preferable to free prayers?

Yes. Because they are not the prayers of the Minister, but of the Church; not of a single congregation, but of the whole Church; and because each person may readily take part in them.

The needs of God's people are ever the same, and the beautiful forms, which the Church has developed in her experience through the ages, give full expression to the believer's wants at all times.

107. Why is the Lord's Prayer used in addition to the General Prayer?

Because no act or service of prayer is complete without it. Christ's direction to His disciples was, "When ye pray, say, Our Father," etc. (Luke 11:2). Luther says, "It is a prayer of prayers, wherein our Lord has comprised all spiritual and bodily need."

108. In the making of announcements, which is allowable at this point, what care should be exercised?

The Minister should avoid making announcements which would suggest thoughts out of harmony with the worship.

The Hymn

109. What is offered next?

The fruit of our lips in a hymn of praise, which properly concludes the Office of the Word.

110. What should be the character of this hymn when the Holy Supper is administered?

It should serve to prepare the hearts of the people for the Service of the Holy Supper, which is now at hand.

111. Should the Holy Supper be omitted?

The Holy Supper should not be omitted. The entire Service is a unit. The omission of the second renders the first part incomplete, since the Holy Supper is the personal application and seal of all that is offered and given in the Office of the Word. The Service without the Holy Supper is like an elaborate feast, during the course of which the guests leave the table before the richest favors are distributed. Very properly is the Service as a whole entitled The Communion.

112. With what should the Service close when the Holy Supper is omitted?

With a hymn or Doxology and the Benediction.

113. What is a Doxology?

The term is derived from two Greek words, *doxa:* glory, and *logos:* a saying. Every ascription of praise to the Triune God is a doxology. The Gloria in Excelsis and the Gloria Patri are known respectively as the Greater and the Lesser Doxology. Following the ancient practice of concluding the Psalms with the Lesser Doxology, we may sing at the end of the closing hymn an ascription of praise to the Trinity in a form of words corresponding with the metre of the hymn.

114. What should be the last act of the worshiper before he leaves the Sanctuary?

He should offer a silent prayer, thanking God for the gift of His grace in this Service, and asking to be kept steadfast in the faith, and to be made fruitful in good works.

A FORM OF SILENT PRAYER.

O God, I thank Thee for Thy gifts of grace; strengthen me, through the same, in faith and in all good works; through Jesus Christ my Lord. Amen.

The Holy Supper

NOTE.—We now come to the most sacred, and solemn act of all Christian worship—the personal communion of the living Saviour with each individual heart. The parts which precede are preparatory to what is about to take place.

The first part, called the Office of the Word, of which the Gospel is the center, is not an independent service. It is the Good News, the forgiveness of sins, proclaimed to all; while in the second part, the Holy Supper, the Good News is applied to each soul.

115. How did the ancients emphasize the peculiar sacredness of this part of the Service?

The first part, a service of teaching, was known as the "Mass of the Catechumens." At its conclusion the Catechumens were dismissed with special prayers. The second part was known as the "Mass of the Faithful." To this, none but communicants were admitted. The doors were closed and guarded, so that no profane eye might behold the sacred Mystery. An old liturgy tells us in what spirit the people must approach the Holy Table: "Let no one have aught against anyone; let no one come in hypocrisy; let us stand upright before the Lord with fear and trembling."

116. What shall be the attitude of the Minister and the Congregation at the beginning of the Holy Supper?

While the hymn is sung, the Minister shall go to the Altar, make ready the Communion vessels, and prepare for the administration of the Holy Communion.   The hymn ended, the Congregation shall rise, and stand to the end of the Agnus Dei.

117. **What are the main divisions of the Office of the Holy Supper?**

    Part I.   The Preface.

    Part II.   The Administration.

    Part III.   The Post Communion.

Part 1.—The Preface

118. **What does the word preface mean?**

    A foreword, an introduction—from the Latin *praefatio,* a saying beforehand.

119. **What is the nature of the Preface?**

    It is a High Thanksgiving.

120. **What are its divisions?**

    1.   The Salutation and Response.

    2.   The Prefatory Sentences.

    3.   The Eucharistic Prayer.

        (a) The Common Preface.

        (b) The Proper Preface.

    4.   The Sanctus.

The Salutation and Response

The Lord be with you.
And with thy spirit.

121. **Where in the Scriptures are the Salutation and Response found?**

    The Salutation is found in Luke 1 : 28, and in Ruth 2 : 4 ; The Response, in II Timothy 4 : 22.

122. To whom is the Salutation spoken?

To the Congregation.

123. What is its purpose?

To greet the worshipers with a blessing; to invite attention; to incite to devotion; and to suggest the coming act of worship.

124. What does the Salutation further imply?

That the Lord must first come to us before we can go to Him; as much as to say, "The Lord be with you and in you and help you to pray." Read Romans 8:26.

125. What is the meaning of the Response?

The people ask a blessing upon the Minister, and pray that the Lord may give him a devout mind, and guide him in the coming ministrations.

The Prefatory Sentences

Lift up your hearts.
We lift them up unto the Lord.
Let us give thanks unto the Lord our God.
It is meet and right so to do.

126. What is the significance of these Sentences?

From the most ancient times these Sentences opened the Service of the Holy Eucharist. They stand in close connection with the Salutation and Response, and give specific direction to the Congregation's devotions which, in view of the exalted nature of the acts of worship which follow, should be full of joy and gratitude.

127. What is the meaning of the first Sentence?

"Lift up your hearts" (Latin, *Sursum corda*) that is: Think of nothing earthly, but arise, go to the very throne of God and offer prayer and praise; for, not only is Christ present in the Sacrament, but He also sits at the right hand of God. This lifting up of hearts finds its fullest expression in the words of the Sanctus.

128. How do the people respond to the Sursum Corda?

They accept the Minister's summons, and answer with assurance, "We lift them (our hearts) up unto the Lord."

129. What is the meaning of the second Sentence?

"Let us give thanks unto the Lord our God" (Latin, *Gratias agamus*), that is: After leading the people to the throne of God, the minister rouses their minds to a sense of His benefits and suggests the nature of the prayer they are to offer.

130. And how do the people take this?

In the Response, "It is meet and right so to do," they accept the thanksgiving thought, and declare their readiness to join in the great Eucharistic Prayer which follows.

The Eucharistic Prayer

IT IS truly meet, right, and salutary, that we should at all times, and in all places, give thanks unto Thee, O Lord, Holy Father, Almighty Everlasting God:

FOR in the mystery of the Word made flesh, Thou hast given us a new revelation of Thy glory; that seeing Thee in the Person of Thy Son, we may be drawn to the love of those things which are not seen.

THEREFORE with Angels and Archangels, and with all the company of heaven, we laud and magnify Thy glorious Name; evermore praising Thee, and saying:

131. What is the nature of the Eucharistic Prayer?

It is a prayer of Thanksgiving—in imitation of our Lord who gave thanks when He took the bread and the cup to institute the Holy Communion. The Church has always said grace, or rendered thanks before partaking of the Holy Supper (I Cor. 10:16). This Thanksgiving was called by the Greeks *Eucharistia,* hence the term Eucharist used for the whole office. The Eucharistic Prayer is the principal division of the Preface, and gives it its chief significance.

132. What should be the posture of the Minister during this prayer?

While offering this prayer, he should by all means face the altar. No one turns his back to the table when he asks the blessing.

133. To whom is the Eucharistic Prayer addressed?

To God the Father.

134. What are the parts of this beautiful prayer?

It is composed of:

1. The *Common Preface,* which consists of two minor parts—
   (a) The General Thanksgiving: "It is truly meet," etc.
   (b) The Conclusion: "Therefore with angels," etc.
2. The *Proper Preface,* which, when used, is inserted between (a) and (b) in the Common Preface.

135. What is the meaning of the General Thanksgiving or first part of the Common Preface?

It is a testimony or acknowledgment to God for *all* His blessings, natural and spiritual. In olden times it was very lengthy, the thought beginning with creation. Read Psalm 26: 6, 7.

136. Explain the Proper Preface?

The Proper Preface is a special thanksgiving to our heavenly Father for the blessing of redemption in Christ Jesus.

137. How does the Proper Preface vary?

With the season of the Church year. It thus brings the Communion Office into close connection with the Service of the Day, and makes each of the chief elements of redemption, in turn, the reason of the Eucharistic Prayer. For example, in the Proper Preface for Christmas, given above, the Incarnation of our Lord is made the leading thought of the Prayer.

138. How do you explain the conclusion of the Eucharistic Prayer?

The conclusion of the Eucharistic Prayer is also the introduction to the Sanctus. Although addressed to God in prayer, it also serves as a summons to all who have "lifted up their hearts" to join heaven's worshipers in singing, as one family, the Seraphic hymn. Read Ephesians 3: 14, 15.

The Sanctus

HOLY, holy, holy, Lord God of Sabaoth; Heaven and earth are full of Thy glory; Hosanna in the highest.

Blessed is He that cometh in the Name of the Lord. Hosanna in the highest.

139. What does the word Sanctus mean?

It is the Latin for *Holy.* Other titles of this hymn are Ter Sanctus and Trisagium, both meaning Thrice Holy.

140. What is the Sanctus?

It is *the great hymn* of the Communion Service—the very climax of the Thanksgiving.

141. What are its divisions and whence derived?

It consists of two verses, of which—

The *first* is from Isaiah the prophet, who heard it sung by the Seraphim before the throne of God. Read Isaiah 6:2, 3.

The *second* was sung by the multitudes which went with Christ on His triumphal entry into Jerusalem (Matthew 21:9). The same words are in the hymn (Psalm 118) which our Saviour is supposed to have chanted with the disciples at the institution of the Holy Supper.

The *first* is heaven's hymn of praise. The *second* is earth's hymn of praise. Thus is fulfilled, "Heaven and earth are full of Thy glory."

Each verse closes with *Hosanna in the highest.*

142. State the nature of the first verse.

It is an exalted strain of praise, in which the saints on earth join the angels in heaven in declaring God's perfection, and in proclaiming that His glory as manifested in Creation and Redemption fills all things. This verse recalls the words of the Eucharistic Prayer, "At all times and in all places."

143. What is suggested by the second verse of the Sanctus?

In the second verse—also called Benedictus—we hail Christ as our Saviour and Deliverer. These words resolve the whole Sanctus into a hymn of praise to Christ as God (John 12:41). We here look forward to the Administration, in which the Lord comes to each one.

144. What is the meaning of Hosanna in the highest?

Hosanna means, Save, I pray.

In the highest, in high heaven.

This expression is an exclamation of the most intense feeling and gives utterance to the loftiest praise.

It is also explained as a cry similar to *God save the King!* What a welcome to Christ our King!

145. Why may the Exhortation, which is inserted at this point in the Service, be omitted?

Because it makes a break in the Service, and this is not the place for preaching.

146. What was the original purpose of the Exhortation?

It was prepared by Volprecht of Nuremberg (1525) for the purpose of teaching the people, who had been reared under Romish error, the true meaning of the Lord's Supper.

147. Why may it be regarded as belonging to the Preface?

Because it is preparatory in character;

Because in some Lutheran Church Orders it took the place of the Preface; and

Because like some of the ancient Prefaces it serves the purpose of teaching.

NOTE.—This truly is the Mass or Service of the Faithful. The guest at the Lord's Table is not so much the poor Publican pleading for mercy, as the justified child of God, who boldly draws near to the throne of grace, lifts up his heart unto the Lord (Prefatory Sentences), gives thanks to his reconciled God (Eucharistic Prayer), and praises Him in exalted strains (Sanctus). Filled with this spirit, Christ's brethren are truly ready to sup with Him.

Part 11.—The Administration

148. **148.** Name the several parts of the Administration.

1. The Lord's Prayer.
2. The Words of Institution.
3. The Pax.
4. The Agnus Dei.
5. The Distribution.
6. The Blessing.

The Lord's Prayer

OUR Father, who art in heaven; Hallowed be Thy Name; Thy kingdom come; Thy will be done on earth, as it is in heaven; Give us this day our daily bread; And forgive us our trespasses, as we forgive those who trespass against us; And lead us not into temptation; But deliver us from evil; For Thine is the kingdom, and the power, and the glory, for ever and ever. Amen.

149. Why does the Minister precede the Lord's Prayer with the words "Let us pray"?

For the reason that, although the Lord's Prayer is recited by the Minister, it is the self-consecratory prayer of *all* the people, as they declare and confirm by singing *Amen* at the close.

150. Why did the early Church introduce this prayer into the Communion Service?

On account of its sacredness.

(a) From ancient times it has always been regarded as a divine and spiritual form of prayer, which can never fail to move our heavenly Father, because His Son taught us thus to pray. On this Cyprian says beautifully: "What prayer can be more spiritual than that which was given us by Christ, by Whom also the Holy Spirit was sent? What petition more true before the Father than that which came from the lips of His Son, Who is the Truth?"

(b) Its use was esteemed the peculiar privilege of *true believers*. Hence it was said, not in the first part of the worship, where we usually have it, but in the Communion Service, from which the heathen and the catechumens (the unbaptized) were excluded. The latter were strictly forbidden to utter it. Chrysostom explains thus: "Not until we have been cleansed by the washing of the sacred waters are we able to call God, Father."

151. Is the Lord's Prayer a part of the Consecration of the Elements?

No. Because such a use does not agree with the nature of the Lord's Prayer, nor with the proper nature of a prayer of consecration, nor with the view of the Ancient Church.

The Words of Institution

OUR Lord Jesus Christ, in the night in which He was betrayed, took bread; and when He had given thanks, He brake it and gave it to His disciples, saying, Take, eat; this is My Body, which is given for you; this do in remembrance of Me.

After the same manner, also, He took the cup, when He had supped, and when He had given thanks, He gave it to them, saying, Drink ye all of it; this cup is the New Testament in My Blood, which is shed for you, and for many, for the remission of sins; this do, as oft as ye drink it, in remembrance of Me.

152. Where are the Words of Institution recorded?

In the Gospels according to St. Matthew 26: 26-28, St. Mark 14: 22-24, St. Luke 22: 19-20, and in St. Paul's First Letter to the Corinthians 11: 23-25.

153. What does our Lord here teach?

I.   The Sacramental Use—"Take, eat," "Drink ye all of it."

II.   The Sacramental Presence—"This is My body," "This cup is the New Testament in My blood."

III.   The Sacramental Benefit—"Which is given for you," "Which is shed for you and for many."

IV.   The Sacramental Institution—"This *do* in remembrance of Me," "This *do*, as oft as ye drink it, in remembrance of Me."

154. What may be said of the Sacramental Use?

Our Lord's words "Take, eat" and "Drink of it" plainly teach that the Sacrament is not complete until used as He directed. As Luther in the Small Catechism says, "The bodily eating and drinking are among the chief things in the Sacrament."

155. What may be said of the Sacramental Presence?

When our Lord said "This is My body" and "This is My blood," He declared unmistakably that when His people eat and drink the sacramental bread and wine, He gives them His true body and blood.

156. What may be said of the Sacramental Benefit?

The words "Given for you" and "Shed for you for the remission of sins" teach:

That Christ takes our place. He suffered death in our stead. That we take His place. We are counted righteous for His sake.

This is the taking away or "remission of sins"—the sacramental benefit which belongs to every communicant who believes Christ's words.

157. What may be said of the Sacramental Institution?

When Jesus said "This do in remembrance of Me," He commanded His people to follow His example by observing the Sacrament, that is, by taking bread and wine, asking a blessing, giving and eating, and thus showing His death till He come.

158. What does St. Paul say about the Sacramental Fellowship?

He teaches that by our communion with the one Lord in this Sacrament we are also brought into the closest fellowship with one another. "For," says he, "we being many are one bread, and one body: for we are all partakers of that one bread." I Cor. 10: 17.

This same thought is beautifully brought out in an ancient Christian writing, called the "Teaching of the Twelve Apostles," belonging to the middle of the second century, as follows: "Even as this broken bread was scattered over the hills, and was gathered together and became one, so let Thy Church be gathered together from the ends of the earth into Thy Kingdom, for Thine is the glory and the power through Jesus Christ forever."

159. Were not Christ's Words intended only for the first administration?

The words which Christ uttered at the Institution made the Holy Supper a sacrament not only for that time, but they endure, have authority, and operate for all time, i. e., "till He come."

160. Why is the recitation of Christ's Words called the Consecration?

Consecration signifies a *setting apart for a holy use.* It is by means of Christ's words that the bread and wine on the altar are set apart for a sacred use; and that the eating and drinking of the bread and wine become a holy ordinance—a sacrament.

161. Why do the rubrics direct the Minister to take the Plate and the Cup when he recites the Consecration?

It is done in imitation of the action of our Lord, Who took the bread and the cup and blessed. Also to show the people that *this* bread and *this* wine are now being consecrated for *this* administration of the Sacrament.

The Pax

The Peace of the Lord be with you alway.

162. What precedes the distribution?

A short benediction called the Pax (Latin for *Peace*). It is the greeting of our risen Lord to His people who are about to approach the altar to partake of His glorified body. Read John 14:27; 20:19, 21.

The Agnus Dei

O CHRIST, Thou Lamb of God, that takest away the sin of the world, have mercy upon us.

O Christ, Thou Lamb of God, that takest away the sin of the world, have mercy upon us.

O Christ, Thou Lamb of God, that takest away the sin of the world, grant us Thy peace. Amen.

163. What is the Agnus Dei?

It is an ancient morning hymn—a modified form of a part of the Gloria in Excelsis, founded on John 1 : 29. Since about the year 700 it has been in use in the Communion Office.

The title of the hymn is taken from the opening words of its Latin form, Agnus Dei, that is, Lamb of God.

164. When should it be sung?

It may immediately precede the Distribution, or more properly, it may be used at the beginning of the Distribution.

165. How is this hymn related to the Sacrament?

In the Words of Institution, which Christ spoke after the supper of the Passover lamb, He announces that through His death He becomes the true Paschal Lamb that takes away the sin of the world. As such we thrice confess Him in the Agnus Dei (John 1 : 29). Read also Exodus 12 : 21-23; I Cor. 5 : 7; I Peter 1 : 19, 20.

166. For what benefit do we ask in this hymn?

We pray here to the Lamb of God, Who is about to impart His body and blood, that He would grant us the mercy and peace which He has obtained for us through His death. Read Ephes. 2 : 13-17.

The Administration

Take and eat, this is the Body of Christ, given for thee.

Take and drink, this is the Blood of the New Testament, shed for thy sins.

The Body of our Lord Jesus Christ and His precious Blood strengthen and preserve you in true faith unto everlasting life.

167. Is this part of the Service important?

It is the most important act in the whole Service, because in it takes place the closest communion between Christ and His people. The believer now reaches the loftiest summit of all worship. He is as near heaven as he can be in this life.

168. What takes place in the Distribution?

The body and blood of Christ are given to the communicants with the bread and wine.

169. What is the purpose of the words used at the Distribution?

The minister thereby calls to the mind of each communicant:
That he is now receiving Christ's body and blood;
That this body and blood were given for his redemption;
That the Gospel promise of forgiveness is now applied.

170. How does the Minister dismiss the communicants from the altar?

The Distribution closes as it began, with a benediction. This blessing also ends the Administration.

171. What is the significance of this benediction?

It is an assurance that the blessed Lord, who has just imparted Himself to His people, will strengthen and preserve the faith with which they received the Sacrament, and without which it would become not a blessing but a curse.

172. If it should happen that the bread and wine on the altar be spent before all have communed, what shall be done?

If the consecrated Bread or Wine be spent before all have communed, the Minister shall consecrate more, saying aloud so much of the Words of Institution as pertains to the element to be consecrated.

Part 111.—The Post Communion

173. What is the third part of the Holy Supper?

The Post Communion, literally, the After Communion, consisting of

    I. The Nunc Dimittis.

    II. The Prayer of Thanksgiving.

    III. The Benediction.

174. What is the general purpose of the Post Communion?

To express our grateful joy for the heavenly food received in the Holy Supper. It is therefore unseemly to leave the House of God, as is frequently done, before offering this Thanksgiving.

The Nunc Dimittis

LORD, now lettest Thou Thy servant depart in peace: according to Thy word;

For mine eyes have seen Thy salvation: which Thou hast prepared before the face of all people;

A light to lighten the Gentiles: and the glory of Thy people Israel.

Glory be to the Father, and to the Son: and to the Holy Ghost;

As it was in the beginning, is now, and ever shall be: world without end. Amen.

175. What is the Nunc Dimittis?

It is a hymn of joyful thanksgiving for the salvation manifested and bestowed in Christ Jesus. It was first used by the aged Simeon when he saw the infant Saviour in the Temple (Luke 2: 29-32). It derives its name from the first words of the Latin version.

176. What is the significance of the Nunc Dimittis here?

It is the closing hymn of the Communion and accords with the practice of our Lord (Matt. 26: 30). That for which the believer has come into the Sanctuary has been received in all its fulness, and he now feels himself at peace with God and declares his readiness to depart.

The Prayer of Thanksgiving

O give thanks unto the Lord, for He is good.
And His mercy endureth for ever.

WE give thanks to Thee, Almighty God, that thou hast refreshed us with this Thy salutary gift; and we beseech Thee, of Thy mercy to strengthen us through the same, in faith toward Thee, and in fervent love toward one another, through Jesus Christ, Thy dear Son, our Lord, Who liveth and reigneth with Thee, and the Holy Ghost, ever one God, world without end. Amen.

177. How is the Prayer of Thanksgiving introduced?

By the Versicle and Response, taken from the opening verses of Psalms 105, 106, 107, 118 and 136.

178. What is the significance of this Versicle?

It is a bidding to the people to unite in the Prayer of Thanksgiving which follows.

179. What is the purpose of the Prayer of Thanksgiving?

Just as we offer thanks after meat, we here express our gratitude to God for the refreshment we have experienced by partaking of His heavenly food. Read John 6: 30-34, 47-58.

We then pray, that this food may enable us to have a right faith toward God and an ardent love toward our fellow men.

The Benedicamus

The Lord be with you.
And with thy spirit.
Bless we the Lord.
Thanks be to God.

180. Why use the Salutation in this place?

It introduces the Benedicamus, and serves to prepare the hearts of the people for the final blessing.

181. What is the significance of the Benedicamus and Response?

The Service now draws to a close with a strain of praise and thanksgiving for the fulness of God's grace which has been unfolded throughout the worship.

NOTE.—In the mediaeval church the words "Bless we the Lord" were sometimes used in place of "Go, you are dismissed" as a formula of dismissal. The same formula closed the Matins when not conducted by an ordained Minister, the benediction being omitted. We also find "Bless the Lord" as a doxology at the close of each book in the Psalter. See Psalm 41:13; 72:18, 19; 89:52; 106:48; 150:6.

The Benediction

The Lord bless thee, and keep thee.
The Lord make His face shine upon thee, and be gracious unto thee.
The Lord lift up His countenance upon thee, and give thee peace.

182. What is the Benediction?

It is the final blessing of the people, commanded by God (Num. 6:22-26), and always regarded by the Church as one of the most solemn parts of the Service. Says an ancient writer: "When the Benediction is pronounced, you should incline both head and body, for the blessing which is given you is the dew and rain of heaven."

183. What is the nature of the Benediction?

It is not a mere pious wish, but is the actual impartation of a blessing from God to the believing congregation, as we are assured in Numbers 6:27, "They (the priests) shall put my name upon the children of Israel; and I will bless them."

Because of the singular pronoun "Thee," it is highly appropriate as the conclusion of the Communion, in which through the Sacrament, the Lord has bestowed His grace upon each believer.

184. Explain more fully the meaning of this solemn blessing.

The first verse—"The Lord bless thee," etc.—offers God's blessing and watchful protection.

The second verse—"The Lord make His face shine," etc.—announces the blessed favor and mercy of God. Our sins have invited the displeasure and frowns of our heavenly Father, but through forgiveness in Christ Jesus communion is restored and God now smiles upon us. Read Isaiah 59:2.

The third verse—"The Lord lift up," etc.—assures us of God's own love. "Lifting up one's countenance or eyes upon another" is an ancient form of speech for "bestowing one's love, for gazing lovingly and feelingly upon another, as a bridegroom upon the bride, or a father upon his son." Having received God's grace in Word and Sacrament, we are now assured of the peace that passeth all understanding.

This we believingly accept in the final

Amen.

[For remarks on the closing silent prayer see Quest. 114.]

The Common Service.

Sketch of the Lutheran Liturgy

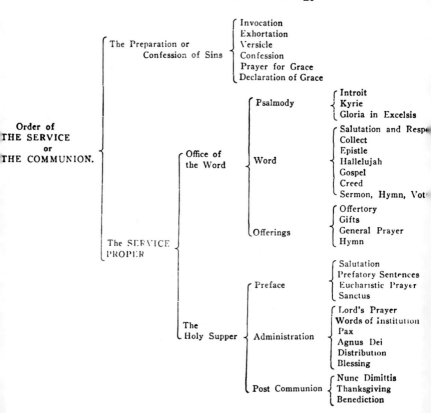

Order of
THE SERVICE
or
THE COMMUNION.

The Preparation or Confession of Sins
- Invocation
- Exhortation
- Versicle
- Confession
- Prayer for Grace
- Declaration of Grace

The SERVICE PROPER

Office of the Word

Psalmody
- Introit
- Kyrie
- Gloria in Excelsis

Word
- Salutation and Response
- Collect
- Epistle
- Hallelujah
- Gospel
- Creed
- Sermon, Hymn, Votum

Offerings
- Offertory
- Gifts
- General Prayer
- Hymn

The Holy Supper

Preface
- Salutation
- Prefatory Sentences
- Eucharistic Prayer
- Sanctus

Administration
- Lord's Prayer
- Words of institution
- Pax
- Agnus Dei
- Distribution
- Blessing

Post Communion
- Nunc Dimittis
- Thanksgiving
- Benediction

Matins and Vespers

Matins and Vespers

The Hours

185. What is the origin of Matins and Vespers?

They can be traced back in the history of the Church to the early Christian observance of the Jewish hours of prayer. Acts 3 : 1; 10 : 9.

186. Which were the hours of prayer observed by the Jews?

The third, sixth and ninth hours of the day (reckoning from sunrise to sunset). Psalm 55 : 17; Daniel 6 : 10.

187. Were additional hours observed by the Christians?

Yes, very early in the history of the Church, six hours of prayer were appointed, then seven, and in the sixth century eight, which is the number still observed in the cloisters of the Roman Church.

188. What reasons did the ancients give for observing these hours of prayer?

They were regarded as commemorative of important events in the life and passion of our Lord, and in the lives of the Apostles.

The Apostolic Constitutions (A. D. 350) mention the hours as follows: "Ye shall make prayer in the morning, giving thanks, because the Lord hath enlightened you, removing the night, and bringing the day; at the third hour, because the Lord then received sentence from Pilate; at the sixth, because He was crucified; at the ninth, because all things were shaken when the Lord was crucified, trembling at the audacity of the impious Jews, not enduring that the Lord should be insulted; at evening giving thanks, because he hath given the night for rest from labor; at cock-crowing, because that hour gives glad tidings that the day is dawning in which to work the works of light."

Another theory beautifully connects them with the acts of our Lord in His passion as follows:

Evensong with His Institution of the Eucharist, and washing the disciples' feet, and going out to Gethsemane; Compline with His agony and bloody sweat; Matins with His appearance before Caiaphas; Prime and Tierce, with that in the presence of Pilate; Tierce also with His scourging, crown of thorns, and presentation to the people; Sext, with His bearing the cross, the seven words, and crucifixion; Nones, with His dismission of His spirit, descent into hell and rout of Satan; Vespers with His deposition from the cross and entombment; Compline with the setting of the watch; Matins with His resurrection.

189. What religious exercises were prescribed for the several hours?

Matins, before day-break, Meditation on the Divine Word, for the reading of which, full and regular provision is made in this hour.

Lauds, at dawn, Praise. As the birds and all nature begin their song, the praise of the Creator and Redeemer breaks forth.

Prime, Supplication, for at this hour man looks forward to the day's work, and again takes up the battle of life.

Tierce, Sext and *Nones,* at 9, 12, and 3 o'clock, Hallowing the day. These hours have the same structure, and with Prime, have divided among them the 119 Psalm; for in the toil and sweat of the day, the soul must again and again be directed to the Divine Word, with which every verse of this Psalm is occupied.

Vespers, at the close of the day, Prayer, praise and thanksgiving. As the believer looks back over the course of the day, he seeks relief from its distractions, toils and cares, and then rejoices in all his blessings, and the riches of the grace of God.

Compline, at night, peculiarly the evening hour of Prayer, in which the Christian looks forward into the night with its terrors and works of darkness, and commits himself and his into the safe hands of his Lord.

190. **What hours of prayer were generally observed at the time of the Reformation?**

While all the canonical hours were observed in the monasteries, only Matins and Vespers were said daily in the principal churches; and in villages and smaller parish churches, even Matins and Vespers were seldom held, except on Sundays and Festivals.

191. **Did the Reformers favor the retention of these Services?**

Yes, Luther commended them, for he found nothing in them but the words of Scripture, and he regarded them as invaluable aids in teaching the Word of God.

For this reason they are the most appropriate forms of devotion for use in Schools, Colleges and Seminaries.

192. **Were these Services adopted without change?**

Minor changes were made. The early Services were combined and known as Matins, the evening Services were combined and known as Vespers. But the four component parts, which characterized these hours of prayer were retained.

193. **Which then are the four major parts of Matins and Vespers?**

Hymnody, Psalmody, Lessons, Prayers.

194. **Which are the minor parts?**

At Matins the Invitatory with the Venite; and at Matins and Vespers the Versicles, Antiphons, and Responsories.

195. **What purpose do these parts serve?**

They introduce, unite and give form to the four major parts, and bring the Services into proper relation with the hour of the day and the season of the Church Year.

Matins

196. **Whence is the word Matins derived?**

It comes from the Latin, *matutinus,* which means *belonging to the morning.*

197. **Of what is Matins composed?**

Of six parts, namely:

   I.   The Opening.
  II.   Hymnody.
 III.   Psalmody.
 IV.   Lessons.
  V.   Prayers.
 VI.   The Conclusion.

198. **What may precede the Opening?**

The opening of Matins may be preceded by a hymn of invocation of the Holy Ghost.

199. **Of what does the Opening of Matins consist?**

  1.   The Versicle, with the Gloria Patri and the Hallelujah.
  2.   The Invitatory, with the Venite.

The Versicle

O Lord, open Thou my lips.
And my mouth shall show forth Thy praise.
Make haste, O God, to deliver me.
Make haste to help me, O Lord.

Glory be to the Father, and to the Son,
and to the Holy Ghost:
*As it was in the beginning, is now,
and ever shall be, world without end.
Amen. Hallelujah.*

200. What is the Versicle?

Psalm verses taken from Psalm 51:15, and Psalm 70:1, respectively.

201. What is the meaning of these verses in this connection?

The first is the preparation for praise; for without the Lord's inspiration we can not hope to approach Him. Therefore we ask Him to open our lips.

In the second, as suppliants, we ask Him to help us to serve Him, and to deliver us from all that may hinder our doing His holy will.

The first is expressive of the opening of the day's worship.

The second looks forward to all things that may be hurtful to us during the day.

202. What concludes the Versicle?

The Gloria Patri and the Hallelujah.

203. Why is the Hallelujah added?

In Scripture the Hallelujah is used with the Psalms of praise, especially Psalms 113-118. It is also the refrain of the great hymn of praise sung in heaven (Rev. 19). The combination *Amen, Hallelujah,* is found in Psalms 106:48, and Rev. 19:4. With the Gloria Patri it strikes, at the very beginning, the key-note of the service—Hallelujah, i. e., Praise ye the Lord!

204. Why is the Hallelujah omitted during the Passion Season?

Because the Passion Season (Septuagesima to Easter Eve) is

the Church's sorrowful commemoration of the sufferings and
death of Jesus Christ; while the Hallelujah is the joyful song
of the Redeemed in praise of the Risen and Glorified Christ.
Read Rev. 19: 1, 3, 6.

The Invitatory and Venite

THE INVITATORY.

O come, let us worship the Lord.
For He is our Maker.

VENITE, EXULTEMUS. PS. XCV.

O COME, let us sing unto the Lord:
let us make a joyful noise to the
Rock of our Salvation.

Let us come before His presence with
thanksgiving: and make a joyful noise
unto Him with psalms.

For the Lord is a great God: and a
great King above all gods.

In His hand are the deep places of the
earth: the strength of the hills is His also.

The sea is His, and He made it: and
His hands formed the dry land.

O come, let us worship and bow down:
let us kneel before the Lord our Maker.

For He is our God: and we are the people of His pasture, and the sheep of His
hand.

Glory be to the Father, and to the Son:
and to the Holy Ghost,

As it was in the beginning, is now, and
ever shall be: world without end. Amen.

205. What is the Invitatory?

It is a summons to praise, used responsively: the one part calling to worship, the other part stating the reason for such worship. The former is almost uniformly the same throughout the Church Year, the latter varies with the season, and makes the central fact of each festival the motive for worship.

206. How is the Invitatory to be used?

The first part, or the whole, of the Invitatory, may be sung or said by the Minister, or sung by a single voice, or by the choir, before the Venite; and after the Venite and Gloria Patri the whole Invitatory shall be sung (Rubric). The Invitatory may therefore be regarded as the antiphon of the Venite.

207. What is the Venite Exultemus?

It is the 95th Psalm, which is always used at Matins with the Invitatory. The words of the common Invitatory are taken from this Psalm, and together they constitute a most fitting and beautiful introduction to the day's first Service of prayer and praise.

NOTE.—It was an ancient custom to prefix one or two Psalms to the first Service of the day, probably in order to allow some little time for the clergy and people to assemble before the Office began. The brethren might enter the church at any time before the end of the second Psalm, which was always the 95th. A writer of the 9th century says, that in his time this Psalm was sung only on Sundays, because during the week the people were unable to attend this Service on account of their work, and therefore there was no need to sing the Invitatory Psalm to call them to church.

The Hymn

208. Is every hymn suitable as "The Hymn" of this Service?

No, "The Hymn" should be appropriate to the time of day and the season of the Church Year.

The Psalm

209. What is the Lutheran custom in the use of the Psalms?

In the Lutheran Church they are sung or said, either in their numerical order, or Psalms 1-109 are used at Matins and 110-150 at Vespers. This is done wherever Matins and Vespers are sung daily.

210. How many Psalms may be used at one Service?

The general custom, derived from Luther, is to use from one to three.

211. How are the Psalms connected with the Church Year?

It is the special office of the *Antiphon* to emphasize the particular fact of salvation which the Season commemorates. Thus, if the 23d Psalm is used at Matins on Septuagesima, the proper Antiphon will be one appointed for the Passion Season; for example, "He was oppressed, and He was afflicted," etc.; but if the same Psalm is used at Vespers in the Easter Season, an Easter Antiphon should be used; for example, "I laid me down and slept," etc. In brief, the Antiphon points out the fact, in the light of which, the Psalm is to be read.

212. How are the Antiphons used?

An Antiphon is used at Matins and Vespers, with the Psalms, the Magnificat, the Nunc Dimittis and the Benedictus. It is used in the same manner as the Invitatory, before and after the Psalm.

213. Why is the Gloria Patri sung at the end of each Psalm?

Because the addition of the Gloria Patri fundamentally distinguishes the use of the Psalter in the New Testament Church from its use in the Synagogue. The Messianic references in the

Psalms Jesus declares to have been written concerning Himself (Luke 24:44), and in the confession of that truth, the
Christian Church has always concluded the Psalms with this
ascription of praise to the Holy Trinity.

Thus the Church perpetuates the confession of the co-eternal
Godhead of our Lord and the Holy Ghost, with the Father,
which was denied in the controversies of the fourth century.

The Lessons

214. What controls the selection of Scripture Lessons for the daily Matins
and Vespers?

The principle that every part of the Scripture suitable for
public reading (besides the Epistles and Gospels of the Church
Year which are read in The Service) should be read in the
course of a year.

NOTE—In our churches, when Vespers alone are in common use, and on Sundays
only, the Lessons read are generally those given in the table, which are selected
for their suitableness for the Day or Festival to which they are assigned.

The Response

O Lord, have mercy upon us.
Thanks be to God.

215. How may the Response be used?

It may be sung or said after each Lesson.

216. How may this be regarded?

As a brief but expressive responsory, an appropriation of the
Divine Word, the burden of which is God's mercy to man, and
the believing acceptance of which always awakens thanksgiving.

The Responsory

(CHRISTMAS.)

THE Word was made flesh and dwelt among us.

And we beheld His glory, the glory as of the Only-Begotten of the Father.

Full of grace and truth.

Verse. In the beginning was the Word, and the Word was with God, and the Word was God.

Full of grace and truth.

Glory be to the Father, and to the Son, and to the Holy Ghost.

Full of grace and truth.

217. What is the office of the Responsory?

It serves to connect the Lessons at daily Matins and Vespers with the Church Year. At the Sunday Services when the selection of the Lessons is controlled by the Church Year, the Responsory emphasizes the leading thought of the passages read, and invites meditation upon them.

218. Of what does the Responsory consist?

It consists of the Responsory Proper, the Verse, which recalls and emphasizes the central thought of the Lessons, and the first part of the Gloria Patri. The last sentence of the Response is repeated after the Verse and after the short Gloria Patri.

219. What was the ancient use of the Responsory?

As Matins and Vespers were altogether liturgical in character, singing alternated with the Lessons. As soon as a lad had intoned his Lesson, the whole Choir followed with the singing of a responsory.

220. What is its use in our Services?

Only one Responsory is sung, and that after the last Lesson. The several editions of the Common Service contain Responsories for the principal Festivals and Seasons of the Church Year. The same Responsory should be used at all the Minor Services of a particular Season.

221. What may be substituted for the Responsory?

A hymn. If this is done the hymn should be appropriate as a response to the Lessons and suitable to the season of the Church Year.

If special choir music is introduced into the Minor Services, it should be used as a Responsory, and must therefore likewise be in harmony with the Lessons and the Season.

The Sermon

The sermon at this place is a Lutheran innovation, due to the overwhelming importance given to the preaching of the Gospel at the time of the Reformation. Before that time, the Canticle followed the Lessons and their Responsories.

The Canticle

TE DEUM LAUDAMUS.

WE praise Thee, O God: we acknowledge Thee to be the Lord.

All the earth doth worship Thee: the Father everlasting.

To Thee all angels cry aloud: the heavens, and all the powers therein.

To Thee Cherubim and Seraphim: continually do cry,

Holy, Holy, Holy: Lord God of Sabaoth;

Heaven and earth are full of the Majesty: of Thy Glory.

The glorious company of the Apostles: praise Thee.

The goodly fellowship of the Prophets: praise Thee.

The noble army of Martyrs: praise Thee.

The holy Church throughout all the world: doth acknowledge Thee;

The Father: of an infinite Majesty;

Thine adorable, true: and only Son;

Also the Holy Ghost: the Comforter.

Thou art the King of Glory: O Christ.

Thou art the everlasting Son: of the Father.

When Thou tookest upon Thee to deliver man: Thou didst humble Thyself to be born of a Virgin.

When Thou hadst overcome the sharpness of death: Thou didst open the kingdom of heaven to all believers.

Thou sittest at the right hand of God: in the glory of the Father.

We believe that Thou shalt come: to be our Judge.

We therefore pray Thee, help Thy servants: whom Thou hast redeemed with Thy precious blood.

Make them to be numbered with Thy saints: in glory everlasting.

O Lord, save Thy people: and bless Thine heritage.

Govern them: and lift them up for ever.

Day by day: we magnify Thee.

And we worship Thy name: ever, world without end.

Vouchsafe, O Lord: to keep us this day without sin.

O Lord, have mercy upon us: have mercy upon us.

O Lord, let Thy mercy be upon us: as our trust is in Thee.

O Lord, in Thee have I trusted: let me never be confounded. Amen.

222. What are the Canticles?

They are those poetical passages found in Holy Scripture (except the Te Deum and Benedicite), but not included in the Book of Psalms, which like the Psalms, have been incorporated into the Services of the Church.

223. Which Canticle is used at Matins?

The Te Deum or the Benedictus. An Antiphon may be sung with the Benedictus.

224. How is the use of the Canticle at this place explained?

After the congregation has been fed with the Word of God in the two-fold form of Psalmody and Lessons, it allows the Word to bring forth fruit, and such fruit appears in the Canticles.

225. What is the Te Deum?

It is a very ancient morning hymn of praise, confession of faith, and petition.

226. Which passage in the Te Deum indicates that it is a morning hymn?

"Vouchsafe, O Lord: to keep us *this day* without sin."

227. Which passage indicates that it is a creed?

From "The holy Church throughout all the world," to "to be our Judge."

228. Why is the Benedictus given as an alternative Canticle?

Originally, the Te Deum was used at Matins (the first hour), and the Benedictus at Lauds (the second hour), but when the Reformers adapted these daily Services to the needs of their times, and decreased the number, Lauds was combined with Matins and the use of the Benedictus was retained.

229. What Creed has been used as a Canticle in this Service?

In place of the Te Deum, our Church (but not the Ancient), also used the Athanasian Creed. This they did, because the Athanasian Creed is, above everything else, a confession of the doctrine of the Trinity. In this connection it is of interest to note that this Creed was known in the Middle Ages as "The *Hymn* of St. Athanasius concerning the Trinity," and "The *Psalm,* Quicunque Vult."

The Prayer

230. Of what does the Prayer consist?

Of the Kyrie, the Lord's Prayer and the Collects.

231. How are these prayers characterized by some Lutheran writers?

The Kyrie is penitential, the Lord's Prayer is filial, the Collects are congregational.

232. Which Collects are generally used?

1. The Collect of the Day, which at the close of the Service once again connects it with the Church Year.

2. The Collect for Grace, an ancient and beautiful prayer for the beginning of the day.

3. Between these, other suitable collects.

233. What other prayers may be used?

The Suffrages or the Litany.

234. What are the Suffrages?

The name is derived from the Latin, *suffragium,* meaning, assent. The Suffrages were probably so called, because in them the people assent by responding to the petitions which are offered. They are the prayers of certain Hours as appointed in the Breviary, as the book was called, which contained the daily Services of the Church. The prayers for Lauds and Vespers were combined and arranged into the *General Suffrages.* The *Morning Suffrages* are the prayers for Prime; the *Evening Suffrages,* those for Compline. The Morning and Evening Suffrages are especially well adapted for family worship. The General Suffrages are for use at Matins and Vespers in the same manner as the Litany.

235. What is the Litany?

The name is derived from the Greek, *litancia,* meaning, an entreating.

In the Middle Ages there were quite a number of "Litanies" in use. The Litany of the Common Service is a translation of Luther's reconstruction of what was known as "The Great Litany of all Saints." Luther considered it "the best prayer on earth after the Lord's Prayer." In its general arrangement the apostolic exhortation (I Tim. 2: 1, 2) can be recognized.

236. How should the Litany be used?

It may be sung responsively by two choirs, or said or sung responsively by Minister and Congregation.

The Benedicamus

Bless we the Lord.
Thanks be to God.

237. How may the Service conclude?

Either with the Benedicamus (when no Minister is present), or with a hymn and the New Testament Benediction.

238. What is the significance of the Benedicamus?

It is an ancient formula of dismissal. We also find it as a doxology at the close of each book in the Psalter.

The Benediction

**The grace of the Lord Jesus Christ,
And the love of God,
And the Communion of the Holy Ghost,
Be with you all. Amen.**

239. Where in the Scriptures are these words found?

In II Corinthians 13:14.

240. What is the significance of these words?

They sum up the fulness of the redemption which flows from the Triune God Whom we worship:

The Grace of Christ, which is the ground of our salvation.

The Love of God, which is the source of our salvation, and

The Communion of the Holy Ghost, by Whom this salvation is applied.

Vespers

INTRODUCTORY NOTE.—As Matins and Vespers are almost identical in composition and structure, and vary only because used at different hours of the day, the questions and answers below treat of Vespers only in so far as this service differs from Matins. In those parts which are common to both, the questions and answers on Matins apply equally to Vespers.

241. **Whence is the word Vespers derived?**

It comes from the Latin *Vesper*, which means *evening, eventide.*

242. **What is the fundamental difference between Matins and Vespers?**

The former is a morning service for the beginning of the day; the latter is an evening service for the close of the day.

243. **In what particulars does Vespers differ from Matins?**

1. There is no Invitatory, and no Invitatory Psalm.
2. The order of the principal parts is not the same.
3. The Hymn is an evening hymn.
4. An evening Versicle is used with the Canticle, which is an evening Canticle.
5. Instead of the Collect for Grace, the Collect for Peace is used at the close of the Prayers.

244. **Why are the Invitatory and Invitatory Psalm not used?**

Because the invitation to worship which is extended at Matins is not only to Matins, but to the entire series of the daily Services which Matins opens, and therefore the repetition of these parts is not necessary at the other Hours.

245. **What is the order of the principal parts at Vespers?**

I.   The Opening.
II. Psalmody.
III. Lessons.
IV. Hymnody.
V.   Prayers.
VI. The Conclusion.

246. How may the difference in the order of parts be explained?

A two-fold consideration seems to have determined this variation.

1. It is not fitting for Vespers to begin with praise (i. e., a hymn before the Psalms and Lessons) because freedom from the entanglements of the world is the first thing to be sought in this Service; after the cares and sins of the day, the Word of God must first prepare the way for praise and prayer. Hence the Lessons precede Hymnody.

2. The hymn at Vespers is brought into close connection with the Canticle because God's Word (Psalms, Lessons and Sermon) awakens thanksgiving and praise (in hymn) as well as acceptance and confession of the truth (in canticle). The Matin Canticle (Te Deum) is both a hymn of praise and a confession of faith, while the Vesper Canticles are regarded as pure responses to God's revelation of grace, and the Church has always sought to supply the elements of thanksgiving and praise by the use of a hymn in connection with the Canticle.

Note.—It is considered proper to use a hymn in connection with the Canticle at Matins also, whenever the Benedictus or the Athanasian Creed is used instead of the Te Deum.

The Magnificat

Let my prayer be set forth before Thee as incense.

And the lifting up of my hands as the evening sacrifice.

MY soul doth magnify the Lord: and my spirit hath rejoiced in God my Saviour.

For He hath regarded: the low estate of His handmaiden.

For behold, from henceforth: all gen-
erations shall call me blessed.

For He that is mighty hath done to me
great things: and holy is His Name.

And His mercy is on them that fear
Him: from generation to generation.

He hath showed strength with His arm:
He hath scattered the proud in the imagin-
ation of their hearts.

He hath put down the mighty from their
seats: and exalted them of low degree.

He hath filled the hungry with good
things: and the rich He hath sent empty
away.

He hath holpen His servant Israel, in
remembrance of His mercy: as He spake
to our fathers, to Abraham, and to his
seed, for ever.

Glory be to the Father, and to the Son:
and to the Holy Ghost;

As it was in the beginning, is now, and
ever shall be: world without end.   Amen.

247. Which Canticles are used at Vespers?

The Magnificat, which was always used at Vespers (the next
to the last Hour) and the Nunc Dimittis, used at Compline (the
last Hour of the day). When Vespers and Compline were
combined the use of both Canticles was retained. The Nunc
Dimittis is evidently the most appropriate for the very close of
the day's worship. (For explanation of the Nunc Dimittis, see
Question 175 and following.) The Magnificat has from earliest
times been used as an evening Canticle, looking back to the
blessings and grace of the day.

248. What is the significance of the Versicle of the Canticle?

It introduces the Christian's evening sacrifice of prayer. The incense and the sacrifices of the Old Testament have forever passed away, but their spirit and essence abide, in supplication and prayer.

𝕿𝖍𝖊 𝕮𝖔𝖑𝖑𝖊𝖈𝖙 𝖋𝖔𝖗 𝕻𝖊𝖆𝖈𝖊

The Lord will give strength unto His people.
The Lord will bless His people with peace.

O GOD, from Whom all holy desires, all good counsels, and all just works do proceed: Give unto Thy servants that peace, which the world cannot give; that our hearts may be set to obey Thy commandments, and also that by Thee, we, being defended from the fear of our enemies, may pass our time in rest and quietness; through the merits of Jesus Christ our Saviour, Who liveth and reigneth with Thee, and the Holy Ghost, ever one God, world without end. Amen.

249. What is the significance of the Versicle of the Collect for Peace?

It gives expression to the security and peace which characterize those who have committed all their interests into God's hands, and who know that they are for ever safe, let the coming night bring what it may.

250. Why is the Collect for Peace appointed to be read at the close of the Prayers?

Just as the Collect for Grace is the most appropriate at the close of Matins, before the Christian goes forth to the day's toils, temptations and dangers, so the Collect for Peace is the most appropriate at the close of Vespers, when the day is over and its work and battles are done. At the beginning of the day we need God's grace for all that is before us; at its close we need His Peace—that peace which the world, now left behind, was not able to give.

[For explanation of the Benedicamus and the Benediction see questions 237 to 240.]

Christian Hymnody

Christian Hymnody

A HYMN is a sacred song. A Christian hymn is one that embodies Christian truth, or gives expression to Christian belief and feeling. "Know ye," asks St. Augustine, "what a hymn is? It is a song with praise of God. If thou praisest God and singest not, thou utterest no hymn. If thou singest and praisest not God, thou utterest no hymn."

There are two kinds of hymns, inspired and uninspired. The inspired hymns are all found in the Holy Scriptures. These are the Psalms and all of the Canticles, except the Benedicite which is found in the Septuagint, but not in the Hebrew Bible, and the Te Deum, which is an ancient Christian hymn.

The inspired hymns are all Hebrew in form. The principal characteristic of Hebrew poetry is the parallelism or responsiveness between the two parts of each verse. For instance, in the second verse of the fifty-first Psalm, we read, "Wash me thoroughly from mine iniquity: and cleanse me from my sin." Here the second clause parallels and balances the first, reproducing the same general idea, but in other words and with a slight variation in the thought. In Psalm 119: 113, the two clauses are sharply antithetical. In Psalm 1: 1, there is a regular progression in the thought. Again, the second clause supplies the reason for what is said in the first, as in Psalm 16: 1, or it may state the results which follow, as in Psalm 23: 1. On account of this parallelism, the psalms should always be rendered antiphonally, whether they be read or chanted, each verse being divided for this purpose by the colon.

With the exception of a few, which are numbered with the Canticles, the uninspired hymns of the Church have taken the form of compositions with metre and rime. In this the Church has followed "the universal promptings of human nature peculiar to no age, which in sacred compositions, as in others, looks for smoothness and ease, for the music of language, for the assistance to memory, and for something to rivet the attention; to which the music may form an harmonious accompaniment."

For a long time the preference of the Church was for the Psalms of the Bible; and it is very probable that before the hymn found its way into the Service, it was in common use among the people. Only gradually, because of its value as a means of spiritual edification, did it win for itself a place in public worship. At first, the popular use of the hymn was confined to the heretics, who employed it in the spread of their false doctrines among the people. In self-defence orthodox writers composed numerous hymns, which finally displaced the songs of the heretics. Many of these ancient compositions are still in use in the East, and some of them, in translated form, throughout the Church.

Early Christian Hymnody

Among the very first composers and users of uninspired Christian hymns were the Syrians, whose language closely resembles if it is not identical with the language which was spoken by the common people of Palestine in the time of our Lord. The Syriac hymnody was rich and full, and in general use for a thousand years and more.

The main stream of Church hymnody, however, takes its rise in the Greek Church of the East. The oldest of all Christian hymns is a Greek hymn of Clement of Alexandria (170-220). The later Greek hymnody reached its zenith at the close of the eighth century.

Latin hymnody originated in, and was derived from, the Greek hymnody of the East. The earliest names which can be connected with any Latin hymns, occur at the beginning of the fourth century. But from the fourth to the sixteenth century, the Latin is the main stream of Christian hymnody. It contains the best of the Greek, and was the inspiration of the majority of the first German hymns. Hundreds of the old Latin hymns, in translated form, are in common use in the Christian Church today.

Influence of German Reformation "The Church hymn, in the strict sense of the term, as a popular religious lyric in the praise of God to be sung by the congregation in public worship, was born with the German Reformation." German hymnody surpasses all others in wealth. The number of German hymns cannot fall short of one hundred thousand. "To this treasury of song several hundred men and women of all ranks and conditions—theologians and pastors, princes and princesses, generals and statesmen, physicians and jurists, merchants and travelers, laborers and private persons—have made contributions, laying them on the common altar of devotion." The treasures of German hymnody have enriched churches of other tongues and passed into Swedish, Norwegian, Danish and modern English and American hymn-books. Luther was the leader in the reformation of the doctrine and the worship of the Church: he was also the first evangelical hymnist. "To Luther belongs the extraordinary merit of having given to the German people in their own tongue, the Bible, the Catechism and the hymn-book, so that God might speak *directly* to them in His Word, and that they might *directly* answer Him in their songs." Luther's example inspired many others to compose evangelical hymns, so that by the middle of the sixteenth century a large number of them were in common use. After the period of the Reformation German hymnody was constantly enriched. Where there are so many famous names which claim attention, space forbids more than the mention of the very greatest hymnist since Luther, Paul Gerhardt (1607-1676). In poetic fertility he greatly surpassed Luther, and his one hundred and twenty-three hymns "are among the noblest pearls in the treasury of sacred poetry." The several English Lutheran hymnals now in use, all contain translations from the principal German hymn-writers of the last four centuries.

Sweden In Sweden, the first evangelical hymn-writers were the two renowned brothers, Olaf and Lars Peterson, the chief assistants of Gustavus in the work of reformation. But the greatest name in Swedish Hymnody is that of Johan Olaf Wallin, who at the beginning of the nineteenth century revised the hymn-book, contributing to it about one hundred and fifty hymns of his own. This book remains in the form in which he brought it out. It is highly prized by the Swedes, and is used everywhere.

Denmark Claus Martenson Töndebinder (1500-1576) was the father of Danish hymnology. He issued what was perhaps the first complete hymnary of the whole North. "The Hymn Book for Church and Home Worship," which is in use in Denmark today, may be traced back through many revised and supplemented editions to Töndebinder's "Handbook" published in 1528.

Norway The Norwegians have in the main followed the lead of Denmark in their hymns. Several hymn-books have been in use in Norway, but the one most generally used is "The Church Hymn-book," edited on the basis of existing books by Magnus B. Landstad (b. 1802) and authorized in 1869. A supplement was added in 1892.

Iceland In Iceland, for a long time, the hymn-book consisted of translations of the earlier hymns of the Danish hymnary. It was published under the name of *Graduale* which was explained to mean *Messu-saungs bok* (The Mass-song Book). The last edition was issued in 1773. A new hymn-book, of the first rank among modern Lutheran hymn-books, appeared in 1886. The Bible Poems of Valdimar Briem (b. 1848), have placed him in the first rank among modern hymnists.

The earlier Scandinavian hymns were doctrinal, but the later are to a great extent expressive of religious sentiments, hopes and fears. Their plaintiveness is very marked, while the strength of their writers' personal faith is undeniable. The blending of the two, as in the illustration below, often produces a most pleasing result. That English hymnody might borrow with advantage from the Scandinavian, is not to be doubted, although at present but few translations are available for use. The following is a specimen, from the Danish poet Brorson, of the style of hymn which largely prevails in the North:

> "I build on one foundation,
>   On Christ who died for me;
> Sheltered by Jesus' passion
>   My soul at rest shall be:
> 'Tis there the life of heaven
>   Poor worthless I obtain;
> Through what my Lord has given
>   The Father's love I gain.
>
> No craft or deep invention,
>   No princely power or might,
> Nor aught that man can mention
>   Of mocking or despite,
> Nor weak nor strong endeavor,
>   Nor want's or sorrow's smart,
> Nor death itself, shall sever
>   My soul from Jesus' heart."

England   "The English hymn singing at the time of the Reformation was the echo of that which roused the enthusiasm of Germany under Luther. The most notable proof of this is found in Coverdale's *Goostly Psalms and Spiritual Songs.*" Most of the book "is a more or less close rendering from the German; and some of the finest hymns are Luther's."

The three Wedderburn brothers, before 1546, published a translation of Luther's hymns into Scotch-English, with a paraphrase of Luther's Catechism. It is interesting to note that, long before Calvinistic versions of the Psalms were sung by the Scotch, they used such renderings of Luther's words as the following:

> "And He, that we should not forget,
> Gave us His Body for to eat
> In form of bread, and gave, as sign,
> His Blood to drink in form of wine;
> Who will receive this sacrament
> Should have true faith and sin repent;
> Who uses it unworthily,
> Receiveth death eternally."

and

> "Our baptism is not done all one day,
> But all our life it lasts identical;
> Remission of our sins endures for aye,
> For though we fall, through great fragility,
> The covenant, once contracted faithfully
> By our great God, shall ever remain,
> As oft as we repent and sin refrain."

Very few original English hymns are of earlier date than the close of the seventeenth century, and the actual development of English hymns began among the Nonconformists, the Baptists and the Independents. Isaac Watts (1674-1748), who lifted English hymns out of obscurity into fame, may justly be called the father of English hymnody. After him, Philip Doddridge (1702-1751) may be mentioned. But the greatest English hymnist, and one of the greatest hymn-writers of all ages, was Charles Wesley (1707-1788). He is said to have written no less than sixty-five hundred hymns, and it is perfectly marvelous how many of them rise to the highest degree of excellence. It is an interesting fact that his brother John's little collection of Psalms and Hymns, which was one of the very first attempts at an English hymn-book, was published at Charlestown, while John Wesley was among the Lutherans in Georgia, in 1737.

At the beginning of the nineteenth century, the use of hymns was still a new departure in the order of divine worship in the Church of England. Until the middle of the century, the Dissenting element made up nearly two-thirds of the total contents of the hymn-books in use in this Church. Since then Church of England writers have greatly added to the number of English hymns, translating many of the best Latin and German hymns and producing many more of original composition.

America America has already produced a large number of hymn-writers. Naturally, English Lutheran hymnody is yet in its infancy. However, the proposed "Common English Hymnal" for Lutheran congregations, contains original hymns by Joseph A. Seiss and Henry E. Jacobs, and translations by Dr. Seiss, Charles Porterfield Krauth, Charles W. Schaeffer and Harriet R. Spaeth.

Office of the Hymn As St. Chrysostom says, "Nothing gladdens the soul like modulated verse—a divine song composed in metre." It was Luther's purpose to inculcate the word of God in the hearts of the people by the use of song. The hymn as such is not intended to be didactic, and yet it is one of the surest means of conveying sound doctrine, and perpetuating it in the Church. St. Paul himself recognized the use of Christian song in teaching (Col. 3: 16). Moreover, it is chiefly by the use of the hymn that the participation of the congregation in public worship is secured. The purpose of the hymn in the Service depends upon its position, although in general it may be said that its principal object is to awaken and stimulate devotion. Doddridge's hymns were sung as the enforcement of his sermons, and were probably given out from the pulpit, line by line. Sometimes the hymn serves as a preparation for what follows, as does the principal hymn in Matins; again it is the form in which the congregation appropriates what has preceded, as in the principal hymn in Vespers. The office of each hymn used in the Common Service, and the kind of hymn to be used, have been indicated at the proper places in this Explanation.

Liturgical Colors

Liturgical Colors

Chief Festivals

I Advent to Christmas Eve..........................Violet

Christmas Eve to the end of the Epiphany season......White

Septuagesima Eve to Shrove Tuesday..................Green

Ash Wednesday to Easter Eve, except Good Friday....Violet

Good Friday ....Black

Easter Sunday to Exaudi, included....................White

Whitsunday Eve to the Eve of Trinity.................Red

Festival of the Holy Trinity and Its Octave..........White

Sundays after Trinity, beginning with the 2d Sunday....Green

Minor Festivals

Reformation Festival.................................Red

General Thanksgiving Days............................Red

Harvest Days..Red

Dedication of a Church..............................Red

Days of Humiliation and Prayer......................Black

The Presentation-Annunciation, St. Michael and All
Angels ....White

Apostles' Days, Martyrs' Day, All Saints' Day.........Red

Commemoration of the Dead and Funerals.............Black

Significance of Liturgical Colors

Violet.—A shade of purple, the color of royalty. It symbolizes the majesty of Christ in His humility. Being a sober, earnest color, it invites to meditation, and has been adopted by the Church for the two great seasons of preparation—seasons of fasting and prayer.

White.—The color of light. Also of those who minister in God's presence—Angels, Rev. 15:6. The Elders, Rev. 4:4. The Saints in heaven, Rev. 7:9, 14. Hence, those who minister in holy things in the Sanctuary may appropriately be robed in white. This color symbolizes Divinity, Dan. 7:9, Matt. 17:2; purity, Rev. 19:8; victory, Rev. 3:4, 5; 6:11.

Green.—The common color of nature, in the freshness of her bloom. Restful to the eye, and widely diffused, it is used by the Church for her common seasons. It is also symbolic of the Christian life, which is the fruit of God's grace, set forth in the services of the Season when nature dons her green vesture and brings forth her best fruits.

Red.—The color of blood and fire. It is symbolical of sin and its atonement. Also of the Church, redeemed by the blood of Christ, and testified by the blood of martyrs. Her faith and zeal are enkindled and perpetuated by the fire of God's Holy Spirit.

Black.—The color of darkness, the absence of light. Symbolical of death, and the deepest sorrow and humility.

Index and Glossary

Index and Glossary

Where the reference is to a page, it is indicated by the letter, p.; otherwise, the number of the question is meant. L. stands for Latin; G. for Greek.

Absolution, The divinely authorized declaration of the forgiveness of sin, pronounced by a minister, upon the confession of a penitent. 39, 40.

Advent, L. *adventus*, a coming. The season from the fourth Sunday before Christmas, to Christmas Eve. A penitential season. Also applied to our Lord's Second Coming at the last day.

Adiaphora, G. "things indifferent." Applied to all those matters of Church government and worship, which are not absolutely binding, since neither commanded nor forbidden by God. This principle is abused by those who ignore the requirements of expediency, unity and good order.

Administration of Communion, 148 to 172.

Agenda, L. "things to be done." A book containing directions and formularies for Church worship, and Ministerial Acts. The word has been so used since the fourth century.

Agnus Dei, 163 to 166.

Aisle, L. *ala*, a wing. A passage way in a church, giving access to the pews. Properly, a lateral subdivision of a church, parallel to the nave.

Alb, L. *albus*, white. A liturgical vestment of white linen, enveloping the person, and reaching to the feet. Probably came from the old Greek and Roman under-tunic. The significance is seen in the priest's prayer before putting it on, "Make me white O Lord," etc. It is worn in some parts of the Lutheran Church.

Alms, G. *eleemosune*, mercy. Material gifts, bestowed upon the poor.

Alms-basin, a vessel into which the minister receives the plates with the offerings.

Alms-chest, a box placed at the entrance of a church to receive gifts for benevolent purposes.

Altar, L. *Alta ara*, high altar. In the Lutheran Church (a) The place for the Sacrament; the Lord's Table, from which is administered the Holy Supper. (b) The place for the Sacrifices which the Christian offers to God, in the form of Prayer, Praise and Thank-offerings. In Reformed Churches, 13.

Altar-card, a printed card containing a portion of the Service, placed on the altar to assist the memory of the Minister.

Altar-cloth, a cover of white linen for the altar, to mark it as the table of the Lord. It should cover the altar, even when there is no communion.

Altar cross, a cross of metal or wood, always standing on the altar. In Reformed churches, 13.

Altar-desk, see Missal-stand.

Altar-ledge, see Ledge.

Altar-rail, see Rail.

Altar Service, that part of the Liturgy which is read from the altar.

Ambo, G. *anabainein,* to ascend. In early and mediaeval churches, a raised platform, surrounded by a low wall, placed in the nave, so as to be near the congregation. From it the Scriptures were read, sermons preached, and important church announcements made. Sometimes there were two ambos, one on the north side for the reading of the Gospel, the other on the south side, for the reading of the Epistle. It has been superseded by the modern pulpit.

Amen, 30, 41.

American hymnody, p. 101.

Angels, G. *aggelos,* a messenger. "Pure and complete spirits, created by God, to be His agents in the administration of creation."

Announcements, in general, 108; of special prayers, 100.

Annunciation, The festival which commemorates the Angel's announcement to Mary of the immaculate conception of our Lord. See the Gospel of the Day, Luke 1:26 to 38. It is celebrated March 25th.

Antependium, L. *ante* and *pendere,* to hang before. A colored and embroidered strip of wool, or silk, one-third as wide as the altar, and hanging for a considerable distance over the front. Its color and design vary with the Season of the Church Year.

Anthem, strictly speaking, the same as antiphon (which see). A selection of Scripture set to music. 75.

Antiphon, a verse used as a key-note to a Psalm or Canticle. It should precede and conclude the Psalmody,

and on Sundays and Festivals precede and follow every Psalm. Announcing the thought of the Season, it should be given out by a solo voice, tenor preferably, or by several of the Choir, before the Psalm, and repeated by the entire Choir after the Psalm.

Antiphon of Introit, 47, 48; of Matin Psalm, 212.

Apocrypha, The, G. *apokruptein,* to hide. Books not admitted into the canon of Scripture. The Jews applied the term to books withdrawn from public use as unfit to read, or because of the mysterious truths they contained. See Canon.

Apostles' Creed, 87.

Apse, G. *apsis,* arch or vault. The altar-recess at the east end of a church.

Ascension Day, L. *Ascensio,* a going-up. The Festival of the Lord's ascension or going-up into Heaven. The fortieth day after Easter.

Ash Wednesday, the first day in Lent. So called from the Roman custom of sprinkling upon the heads of the people, the ashes of palm branches consecrated on Palm Sunday of the previous year. The 46th day before Easter.

Athanasian Creed. One of the three general creeds of the Church. It was not written by Athanasius, but is a statement of the doctrine of the Trinity, which he so successfully defended. 229.

Augustine on Hymn, p. 95.

Ave Maria! L. *Hail, Mary!* The salutation which the Angel addressed to the Virgin Mary when he announced the Incarnation. See Luke 1:28.

Bands, An appendage to the collar, worn by clergymen, lawyers, and students. It consists of two broad strips of linen, united above, but separated below, tied about the neck, and worn in front over the robe. It is without any churchly significance, being a relic of the large ruff or collar worn in the sixteenth and seventeenth centuries.

Banns, the proclamation in church of an intended marriage, made to secure for the contracting parties the prayers of the congregation, and as a safeguard against an unlawful union. The word is from the French, *ban,* a proclamation.

Benedicamus, in the Communion, 180, 181; at Matins and Vespers, 237, 238.

Benediction in the Communion, 182 to 184; at Matins and Vespers, 230, 240.

Benedictus, L. for "blessed." The song of Zacharias, Luke 1:68-79. At Matins, 228; B. in the Sanctus, 141, 143, 144.

Bidding Prayer, so called because the Deacon *bids* the people pray, and mentions the things to be prayed for, whereupon the Minister reads the collect, and the congregation responds with the Amen. By ancient usage this prayer was specially appointed for Good Friday.

Brasses, engraved memorials on *brass,* placed in the walls and floors of churches.

Breaking of Bread, A Scripture name for the sacrament of the Holy Supper. In the early Church, fellowship in Christ was symbolized by the use of one loaf, 158.

Brorson, hymn of, p. 99.

Calvin's Service, 13.

Canon, G. Kanōn, a rule or measure. The divine standard of faith and life, given in the inspired writings of the Old and New Testaments. See Apocrypha.

Cantate, L. for "Sing." Fourth Sunday after Easter. Named from the first word in the Introit.

Canticle, L. *Canticulum,* a song. The Canticles are the Te Deum, Benedictus, Magnificat, and Nunc Dimittis. This is also the title of the Song of Solomon, the twenty-second book of the Old Testament. 222 to 229, 247, 248.

Cantor, a church official who instructs in singing, and directs the music of the Service.

Cassock, Perhaps from the Italian *casaeca,* a great coat. A long, close-fitting garment worn by clergymen, with or without other robes, and by choristers under their cottas. Its color may vary with the Festivals. It was originally the common dress of laymen.

Catholic, universal. The term is used in the Athanasian Creed. Wrongly appropriated to themselves by Romanists.

Chalice, L. *calix,* a cup. The cup used in administering the wine in the Supper.

Chancel, L. *cancellus,* chancel; *cancelli,* latticework. The space in a church surrounding the altar, separated from the choir.

Chant, the musical recitation of a psalm or canticle.

Chasuble, L. *casula,* the chief garment of a priest while conducting worship. It is worn outside all other garments, and falls nearly to the knees. It was likely derived from a Roman civil garment. At one time it symbolized the mantle of Charity, but in the present Roman Missal, the yoke of Christ. It is worn in some parts of the Lutheran Church.

Choir, L. *Chorus* (a) a body of singers; (b) the part of a church allotted to the choristers, which in ancient churches was between the chancel and the nave, or body of the church building.

Choir music, special. 75, 221.

Chorister, a singer in a choir.

Chrysostom, St. on the hymn, p. 101.

Christmas, Christ's Mass, or Festival. The Day which commemorates the birth of Christ.

Church, The, The Body of Christ, 158.

Church Year, the year arranged by the Church, for the commemoration of our Lord's life, and for the celebration of great events in the history of the Church and the setting forth of the Christian life.

Cincture, L. *cinctura*, girdle. A belt or girdle worn over the cassock or the alb. Its color may vary with that of the other vestments. It is symbolical of self-restraint.

Clergy, G. *kleros*, a lot; then an office allotted; then those to whom the office was allotted. The body of ministers, collectively.

Collect, analyzed, 64; antiquity, 67, 68; for Peace, 250; of the Day, 61 to 69; at Matins, 231, 232; structure, 63; wide use, 69.

Colors, p. 104, 105.

Common Preface, 134, 135, 138.

Common Service, 19 to 23; names of, 23.

Compline, L *completorium*, completion, 189.

Confession of Sins, 37.

Confiteor, L. meaning, "I confess." The title of the Confession of Sins, so called because at one time it was the confession of the Priest or Minister, and began with this word.

Consecration, The act of setting apart for a sacred use. In the Holy Supper, 160; The Lord's Prayer not a part of, 151, 172.

Corporal, L. *corporale*, pertaining to the body. A square of fine linen,

embroidered on the edge only, placed on the altar under the communion vessels at the Holy Supper.

Corruption of Christian Worship, 11.

Cotta, Cota, L. for tunic, coat. A loose white linen garment worn over the cassock in the choir, and in the administration of the sacraments. Originally it was worn by laymen.

Coverdale's hymn book, p. 100.

Creed, 82 to 87.

Crucifix, A cross or representation of a cross, with the figure of Christ upon it.

Cultus, L. for worship. The form and manner of worship, e.g. the Lutheran C. The C. of the Greek or Roman Church, etc.

Cycles of the Church Year. The three main seasons of the Christian calendar, namely. The Christmas C., the Easter C., and the After Trinity C. The last cycle may properly be called the Post-Pentecostal cycle, since in the old Missals its Sundays are numbered "after the Octave of Pentecost," and its lessons deal with the Christian life as the fruit of the Spirit given on Pentecost.

Danish name of Service, 24; hymnody p. 98.

Deacon, G. *diakonos*, a servant. In the Lutheran Church, a man set apart to assist the Minister in the administration of the temporal affairs of the congregation. The origin of the office is found in Acts 6:1-7.

Deaconess, in the early church, a woman chosen and consecrated to works of love and mercy among the sick, the ignorant, the fallen, the friendless. The office was revived by Fliedner, in Germany in 1836, and introduced into America by

Index and Glossary.

Rev. W. A. Passavant, D.D., in 1849.

Declaration of Grace 39, 40.

Distinction between the several Services, 23.

Distribution, 167-172 .

Doddridge, Philip, hymns, p. 101 and p. 102.

Dorsal, (Dossal), L. *dorsum,* back. A hanging above and behind the altar.

Doxology, 113.

Eagle, a form of lectern, so called because the book-rest is a figure of this king of birds. The eagle is the symbol of St. John.

Early Christian Hymnody, p. 96.

Easter, from the Saxon root *urstan,* rise (supposed). The highest and most joyous day in the Christian year, commemorative of our Lord's resurrection. Called Pascha in the early Church, from the Hebrew, Pesach, the Paschal feast.

Easter Rule. Easter Day is the first Sunday after the full moon which happens on or next after March 21. If the full moon happens on a Sunday, Easter will be the following Sunday.

Elder, in some Lutheran congregations, a member of the Church Council, chosen because of the experience and dignity which age confers.

Elements, the bread and wine in the Holy Supper.

Elements of Minor Services, 193 to 195.

Elevation of the Elements, 161.

England, Church of, hymnody, p. 101.

English Hymnody, p. 100.

English Reformers' Service 16.

Epiphany, G. *epiphaneia,* manifestation. Formerly the Festival of the Nativity, as in the Greek Church today. It is now in the West, the Festival of Christ's manifestation to the Gentiles (Magi). The Ep. Season sets forth the glory of Christ as the Royal Redeemer.

Episcopal (Anglican) worship, 15.

Epistle, The, 70 to 76.

Epistle Corner, or Horn, The right or south-west corner of the altar as you face it.

Epistler, One who reads the Epistle in the Service.

Eucharistic Prayer, 131 to 138.

Evangelists, G. *euaggelistes,* the bringer of good tidings. The writers of the Four Gospels, St. Matthew, St. Mark, St. Luke, and St. John.

Eve, a short form of even, evening. The day and night before a holy day marked by religious and popular observances.

Exaudi, L. "Hear". Sunday after Ascension, named from the first word in Introit of the Day.

Excommunication, an act of Church discipline, whereby the person against whom it is pronounced is cast out of the communion of the Church.

Exercises, for the Hours, 189.

Exhortation, in the Communion, 145 to 147; in the Preparation, 33.

Fast, (a) abstinence from food, as a religious observance; (b) a time of fasting. The principal fasts of the Church are Advent and Lent.

Fastnacht, German, fastnight, the night before the Lenten season begins. English, Shrove Tuesday, which see (Fat Tuesday); French, Mardi Gras, still celebrated in New Orleans. The day before Ash Wednesday—universally a day of carnival and feasting.

Feria, In the old church calendar, any day of the week from Monday to Friday.

Festival of the Church, a day or

calendars. It is also used for Maundy Thursday, which see.

Holy Week, the week beginning with Palm Sunday.

Hours, The, 185 to 195; origin 185; Jewish, 186; early Christian, 187 to 189; at the Reformation, 190 to 192; present, 192.

Hosanna, in the Sanctus, 144.

Host, L. *hostia,* sacrifice. The consecrated wafer in the Holy Supper.

Hymn, defined, p. 95; office in Liturgy, p. 101; before the Service, 28; before the Sermon, 88, 89; closing the Office of the Word, 109, 110; on Communion Days, 110; at Minor Services, 208, 221.

Hymnody, Christian, p. 95-102.

Icelandic hymnody, p. 99.

IHS, the Latinized form of the first three letters in the Greek name Jesus.

Immovable Festival, one which always falls on the same day of the month, irrespective of the day of the week, e.g. Christmas.

Incarnation, L. *incarnatio,* made flesh; the divine act by which the Son of God became man.

Inspired hymns, p. 95.

Installation, the act of inducting an ordained minister into office as the pastor of a congregation, or of any church official into office.

Introduction to the Explanation, p. 9-15.

Introit, 45 to 50.

Invitatory, L. *Invitatorium,* an invitation to the people to praise, 205, 206; why omitted at Vespers, 244.

Invocation, L. *invocatio,* a calling upon. (a) applied to the words, "In the Name of the Father," etc. (b) the first petitions of the Litany. 29; Hymn of In. before Matins, 198; before The Service, 23.

Invocavit (Invocabit), L. for "He shall call." The first Sunday in Lent, named from the first word of the Introit of the day.

Jubilate, L. for "Rejoice." Third Sunday after Easter, named from first word of Introit of the Day.

Judica, L. for "Judge." Fifth Sunday in Lent, named from first word of Introit of the Day.

Kneeling in Prayer. The usual attitude of early Christians in prayer was standing. It was believed to be an apostolic usage in worship. The Council of Nice (325) forbade kneeling on Sundays and in daily worship between Easter and Pentecost.

Knox's Service, 13.

Kyrie at Matins, 230, 231; in Service 51 to 54.

Laetare, L. for "Rejoice." Fourth Sunday in Lent. Named from the first word of the Introit of the Day.

Landstad, Magnus B., p. 98.

Latin hymnody, p. 97.

Lauds, L. *laudes,* praises, 189.

Lavabo, L. *lavare,* to wash. A cloth used in cleansing the rim of the communion cup. Originally, the maniple served a similar purpose.

Lay-Baptism, baptism administered in a case of necessity by one who is not an ordained Minister. If the child lives, the baptism should be confirmed in church.

Layman, L. *laos,* one of the people, as distinguished from the clergy.

Lection, L. *lectio,* "a reading." A lesson from the Scriptures. See Lesson.

Lecturn, G. *lektron,* a book-rest. A reading-desk in a church. A survival of the ancient ambo. Which see.

Ledge, Altar. A step or ledge at the

back of the altar, and raised slightly above it, to receive lights, flowers, etc. Also doubtfully called retable.

Lent, from an Anglo-Saxon word meaning "Spring." The season of preparation for Easter, and commemorating Christ's sufferings. Observed among the ancients by fasting and prayer. Beginning Ash Wednesday it continues forty days, the Sundays not being counted, as they are not fast-days.

Lesson, a portion of Scripture appointed to be read in the Services of the Church, or in private devotions. Lessons in the Service, 70, 71; at Matins and Vespers, 214.

Litany, 235, 236.

Liturgical Colors, p. 104, 105.

Liturgical Vestments, see Vestments.

Liturgy, G. *leitourgia,* public service or duty, (a) a form or method of conducting public worship, (b) the Church Service. Plan of, p. 68.

Lord's Prayer, in Communion, 149 to 151; in Minor Services, 230, 231; in General Prayer, 107.

Luther, Catechism sung in Scotland, p. 100; the earliest reviser of the Service, 17; hymnody, p. 97.

Lutheran Service, older than the Episcopal, 16.

Magnificat, L. for magnifies, in the sense of praises. Sung by the Virgin Mary upon her visit to Elizabeth, Luke 1:46-55. One of the Vesper Canticles, p. 88.

Maniple, L. *manus,* hand and *plenus,* full. Originally a strip of fine linen attached to the left arm of the priest with which to wipe the chalice. See Lavabo.

Marriage Ring, The, was used before Christian times by the Romans. St. Isidore of Seville (d. 636) says the ring was put on the fourth finger of the left hand, because it contains a vein immediately connected with the heart.

Martyrs' Days, G. *martyr,* witness. Days commemorating the death of those who suffered as witnesses for Christ and His religion.

Mass, L. *missa,* dismissal, missa being one of the words in the phrase of dismissal of the congregation, the word then came to denote the particular service from which the people were dismissed. It is used for the Holy Communion, the Service of Communion, and in the names of Church Festivals as Christmas.

Mass, of the Catechumens, 115; of the Faithful, 115.

Matins, 196 to 240.

Matins and Vespers, 185 to 250; distinguished, 242, 243.

Maundy Thursday, Thursday in Holy Week, incorrectly called Holy Thursday, which see. So called, either because it was the day of Feet-washing, from the words of the first antiphon sung during the ceremony, "Mandatum novum," "A new commandment"; or, from the L. Dies Mandati, Day of the Command, commemorating Christ's institution of the Holy Supper when he said, "Do this"; or from the custom of delivering gifts to the poor in baskets (maunds).

Misericordias, L. for mercy. Second Sunday after Easter. Named from the first word in the Introit of the Day. Misericordia is the more correct form of this name.

Missal, from *Missa,* mass. A book containing the Service of the Mass.

Missal-stand. A small desk on the Altar to support the Service-book or missal.

Mortar-board. Probably from the French, *mortier,* the cap worn by the ancient kings of France, and still worn there by officials in Courts of Justice. A popular term for the academic cap, worn at colleges. It has recently come into vogue as the proper head-covering for female choristers.

Movable Festival. One which always falls on the same day of the week, irrespective of the day of the month, e. g., Easter.

Music in Reformed Churches, 13.

Names of the Service, 24.

Nave, L. *navis,* a ship. The middle part, lengthwise, of a church, extending from the entrance to the choir or chancel.

Nicene Creed, 85, 86.

Non-conformist hymnody, p. 100.

Nones, L. *nona,* ninth. 189.

Norwegian, name for the Service, 24; hymnody, p. 98.

Nunc Dimittis, 175, 176; at Vespers, 249.

Octave, L. *octavus,* eighth. The eighth day from a Festival, the feast day being counted as the first, e. g., the Octave of Easter is the I Sunday after Easter. It may also include the intervening days. The celebration of the Festival continues throughout the Octave.

Oculi, L. for eyes. Third Sunday in Lent. So called from the first word in the Introit.

Offerings of Money, 96, 99.

Offerings, Part III of Office of the Word, 94 to 110.

Offertory, 97 to 99.

Office of the Word, 43 to 114.

Omission, of Hallelujah, 51; of Holy Supper, 111, 112.

Opening of Matins, 199 to 207.

Order of Parts of Vespers, 245, 246.

Origin of use of Hymns, p. 96.

Ordinance, L. *ordinare,* to order. An observance which has been commanded, e. g. the Sacraments, Prayer, etc.

Ordination, the official commission and consecration of a Minister of the Gospel by the Church.

Orientation, of a church, the act of placing it so as to have the chancel point to the east (orient); of a minister, the act of turning to face the altar, during the sacrificial parts of the Service.

Palmarum (Palm Sunday) L. for Palms. Sixth Sunday in Lent, named from an old Latin title, "Dominica palmarum" or "Dies palmarum," the Lord's Day of Palms.

Paraments, L. *parare,* to prepare. Church vestments and furniture.

Passion Sunday, the fifth in Lent. It begins the more solemn part of our Saviour's Passion.

Passion Week, the week before Palm Sunday. It is so called in the Breviary.

Paul, St., on the hymn, p. 101.

Paten, the plate which holds the bread used at the Holy Supper.

Pax, 162.

Pentecost, G. word, meaning fiftieth. Another name for Whitsunday, it being the fiftieth day after Easter.

Pericope, G. word, meaning section. Applied to the sections of the Gospels and Epistles selected to be read as the fixed lessons of the Sundays and Festivals.

Peterson, Olaf and Lars, p. 98.

Pew. An enclosed seat in a church.

Plain Chant, see Gregorian Music.

Plan of Liturgy, p. 68.

Post Communion, 173 to 184.

Prayer, at Matins, 230 to 236; for Grace, 38.

It closes the Easter cycle, and the first half of the Church Year. Its celebration was appointed by Pope John XXII in 1334, on the Octave of Pentecost, probably because the outpouring of the Holy Ghost on Pentecost completed the revelation of the tri-unity of God. The choice of the Gospel of this Sunday was probably controlled by the fact that it was the Octave of Pentecost.

Trisagion, G. meaning "three holy." An ancient metrical Greek hymn. It is often confounded with the Seraphic Hymn.

Trisagium, See Seraphic Hymn.

Uninspired hymns, p. 96.

Veil, a square of the finest linen procurable, delicately embroidered with a cross in the middle of one edge. It is used to cover the communion vessels, before and after the Administration.

Venite, L. meaning "Come." The title of the XCV Psalm. 207.

Verba, L. for "Words." Applied to Christ's Words of Institution in the Holy Supper, which see.

Versicle, L. *Versiculus,* a little verse. Of Canticle at Vespers, 248; of Collect for Peace, 249; in Opening of Matins and Vespers, 199 to 202; in Post Communion, 177, 178; in the Preparation, 34 to 36.

Vespers, 241 to 250.

Vestments in the Lutheran Church, are worn by ministers to distinguish them from the non-official members of the congregation, especially the black "chorrock" or academic gown, which is the robe of the teacher rather than of the priest, and which is without any of the sacerdotal significance which

attaches to the vestments of the Roman Church. See bands, cassock, alb, surplice, chasuble, stole, cotta, cincture.

Vigil, L. *vigilia,* a watching. In general, an eve which is a fast. The day and night preceding a Festival.

Visitation, July 2. A festival commemorating the Virgin Mary's visit to St. Elizabeth, after the annunciation. Luke 1:39ff.

Votum, 92, 93.

Wafer, the communion bread, made of fine flour, and unleavened. Usually stamped with a figure of Christ crucified or with the I H S.

Wallin, John O., p. 98.

Watts, Isaac, p. 100.

Wedderburn, hymn-book, p. 100.

Wesley, Charles, p. 101; John, p. 101.

Whitsunday, From White-sunday, the day when the catechumens were robed in white; or Whitsun-day, German Pfingsten-Tag; or Whitsunday, when the Holy Spirit gave wisdom (wit). The Day which commemorates the outpouring of the Holy Spirit upon the Church. See the Epistle of the Day.

Word, Office of the, 43 to 114.

Words of Distribution, purpose of, 169.

Words of Institution, 152 to 161.

Worship, defined, 1; before Christ, 3; after Christ, 3; Christian, 4; Elements of, 5; False, 2; Heathen, 2; Jewish, 2, 3; True, 2.

Year of the Church, the year beginning the fourth Sunday before Christmas (I Advent), appointed by the Church to commemorate the great facts of our Lord's life and work, and the various phases of the Christian's life.

Zwingli's Service, 13.

Laus Deo!

CPSIA information can be obtained
at www.ICGtesting.com
Printed in the USA
FFOW01n2307090116
20181FF